Contents

Welcome to Our Kitchen

When you cook with a Better Homes and Gardens® cookbook, you can be confident that every recipe will taste great every time. That's because we perfect every recipe in our Test Kitchen before we present it to you.

All of us who work in the Better Homes and Gardens® Test Kitchen cherish the moments when our families gather around the dinner table at home.

Just like you, we face the challenge of preparing family-pleasing meals despite long hours away from home. After a day of testing recipes, we appreciate a fuss-free supper that's quick and easy to serve. Crockery cooker meals are perfect choices for such nights.

Knowing you want crockery recipes that go together quickly, we looked for ways to shortcut preparation times. We also made sure that all of the ingredients are available in local grocery stores. Throughout the book we share with you tips that make mealtime in our own homes simpler and more enjoyable.

To ensure that you will obtain the same delicious results in your home that we achieved in the Test Kitchen, we tested recipes in a variety of crockery cookers from different manufacturers such as Rival, Hamilton Beach, and West Bend, and in a range of sizes. For healthwise cooks, we included a selection of low-fat recipes noted with this symbol ♥. Each of these recipes contains no more than 12 grams of fat per serving.

With our heartfelt wishes for many pleasant dinner hours in your home, we present this collection of richly satisfying crockery cooker dinners. Relax and enjoy!

Lynn Blanchard

Lynn Blanchard
Better Homes and Gardens®
Test Kitchen Director

Secrets to Success

Of all the appliances in a kitchen, the crockery cooker is one of the easiest to use. However, even with the cooker's intrinsic simplicity, questions often arise. Here are answers to some frequent questions about the use and care of crockery cookers.

Q.

What is a crockery cooker and how does it work?

A.

All of the recipes in this book were tested in a continuous slow cooker. This appliance slowly and continually cooks food at a very low wattage. The heating coils, or elements, wrap around the sides of the cooker and remain on. On this type of cooker you'll notice fixed settings: low (200°), high (about 300°), and in some models, automatic (shifts from low heat to high heat). The ceramic liner may or may not be removable. Another type of cooker, an intermittent cooker, is not recommended for the recipes in this book. In this cooker, the heating element or coil is located below the food container and cycles on and off during operation. If your cooker has a dial indicating temperatures in degrees, you have an intermittent cooker. Because the recipes in this book need continuous slow-cooking temperatures, an intermittent cooker will not cook the food properly.

Q.

Do crockery cookers come in different sizes?

A.

Crockery cookers range in size from 1 to 6 quarts. Each recipe in this book lists the recommended size or sizes that will accommodate that recipe. Check the capacity of your cooker to see whether it fits the recommendation. For best results the crockery cooker must be at least half full and no more than two-thirds full.

Q.

How often do I need to stir?

A.

For most recipes, you do not need to stir, and stirring can even be harmful. Because a crockery cooker cooks food at a low temperature, removing the lid can dramatically reduce the cooker's interior temperature. Therefore, when you lift the lid to stir or add ingredients, replace it as quickly as possible, especially when cooking on the low-heat setting. An uncovered cooker can lose up to 20 degrees of cooking heat in as little as 2 minutes. A quick peek, however, will change the temperature by only 1 or 2 degrees. To keep the temperature constant, resist lifting the lid.

Q.

Should I use the high-heat setting or the low-heat setting?

A.

If you want dinner to cook all day, use the low-heat setting of your cooker. This allows most foods to cook for 10 to 12 hours. For a shorter cooking time, use the high-heat setting, which cooks most foods in 3 to 6 hours. Cooking times may vary depending on the cooker, but the timings generally work well for all continuous slow cookers. If a recipe recommends cooking only on one setting, do not use any other setting because your food may not turn out properly.

Q.

How do I clean my crockery cooker?

A.

Always remember to unplug your cooker before cleaning and never immerse the cooker or the cord in water. To clean the cooker's ceramic lining, use a soft cloth and warm, soapy water. If your cooker has a removable liner, you can wash it in the dishwasher. Avoid using abrasive cleaners and cleansing pads. To avoid cracking the crockery insert, cool the cooker or the insert completely before cleaning.

Q.

My 6-quart crockery cooker makes more food than my family can eat at one meal. What can I do with the leftovers?

A.

Freeze the leftovers. Many cooks buy large-capacity crockery cookers so they can cook once and have enough leftovers for another meal. To freeze leftovers, cool the food about 30 minutes and transfer it to freezer-safe containers. Label and freeze. To reheat, do not use your crockery cooker. Place the frozen food in an appropriate-size saucepan; cook and stir over low heat until boiling.

playing it safe

Foods prepared in a crockery cooker are safe to eat even though they cook at a very low temperature. The long cooking time and the steam that forms in the tightly covered container destroy any bacteria. To ensure that your food is safe to eat, take a few precautions. Clean the cooker and all utensils before you start. Always completely thaw raw meat or poultry before adding it to the cooker. Do not use the crockery cooker for large pieces of meat. Cut in half any roasts larger than 2½ pounds.

Soups &
Stews

Autumn Harvest Stew

In This Chapter:

Hearty Beef Chili ♥

With an electric crockery cooker, a traditional-style chili made with chunks of beef or pork is as easy to prepare as the more familiar ground beef version.

Prep: 20 minutes **Cook:** 8 to 10 hours plus 15 minutes **Serves:** 10

1 28-ounce can tomatoes, cut up
1 10-ounce can chopped tomatoes and green chili peppers
2 cups vegetable juice or tomato juice
1 to 2 tablespoons chili powder
1 teaspoon ground cumin
1 teaspoon dried oregano, crushed
3 cloves garlic, minced
1½ pounds beef or pork stew meat, cut into 1-inch cubes
2 cups chopped onion
1½ cups chopped celery
1 cup chopped green sweet pepper
2 15-ounce cans black, kidney, and/or garbanzo beans, rinsed and drained
Toppers such as shredded cheddar cheese, dairy sour cream, thinly sliced green onion, snipped cilantro, thinly sliced jalapeño peppers, and/or sliced pitted ripe olives (optional)

1 In a 6-quart crockery cooker combine both cans of undrained tomatoes, vegetable or tomato juice, chili powder, cumin, oregano, and garlic. Stir in meat, onion, celery, and sweet pepper.

2 Cover and cook on low-heat setting for 8 to 10 hours or on high-heat setting for 4 to 5 hours.

3 If using low-heat setting, turn to high-heat setting. Stir in the beans. Cover and cook for 15 minutes more on high-heat setting. Spoon into bowls. If desired, serve with toppers.

Nutrition Facts per serving: 224 cal., 6 g total fat (2 g sat. fat), 49 mg chol., 807 mg sodium, 24 g carbo., 6 g fiber, 24 g pro.
Daily Values: 16% vit. A, 66% vit. C, 7% calcium, 28% iron

Beef and Fresh Mushroom Stew

A medley of mushrooms makes this sherry-flavored soup extra special. If using shiitake mushrooms, remove and discard the tough stems before slicing the caps.

Prep: 20 minutes **Cook:** 8 to 10 hours **Serves:** 6

4 cups sliced assorted fresh mushrooms, such as button, crimini, and shiitake

3 medium carrots, cut into ½-inch slices (1½ cups)

1 cup sliced celery

1 6-ounce package long grain and wild rice mix

1 pound beef stew meat, cut into 1-inch cubes

6 cups beef broth

½ cup dry sherry

1 In a 4- to 6-quart crockery cooker place mushrooms, carrots, celery, and rice mix with seasoning packet. Place meat on top of vegetables. Pour broth and sherry over all.

2 Cover and cook on low-heat setting for 8 to 10 hours or on high-heat setting for 4 to 5 hours.

Nutrition Facts per serving: 279 cal., 5 g total fat (2 g sat. fat), 43 mg chol., 1,394 mg sodium, 30 g carbo., 2 g fiber, 24 g pro.
Daily Values: 77% vit. A, 8% vit. C, 2% calcium, 20% iron

marvelous mushrooms

Varieties of mushrooms have mushroomed in recent years. Today you'll find several types in supermarket produce aisles. The white or brown mushrooms often called button mushrooms are readily available and very mild in flavor. Morels, shiitakes, and portobellos offer a richer, earthier flavor.

The best way to clean all types of mushrooms is to brush them with a clean, soft vegetable brush and wipe them with a clean, damp cloth. Do not soak mushrooms or run them under water because they will soak up water like sponges, ruining their texture.

Beef Bourguignon

This classic French stew becomes weekday fare when cooked in the crockery cooker. Serve with a loaf of crusty French bread and a simple salad of mixed greens and vinaigrette.

Prep: 40 minutes **Cook:** 10 to 12 hours **Serves:** 6

1 pound boneless beef chuck roast, cut into ¾-inch cubes
2 tablespoons cooking oil
1 large onion, chopped
1 clove garlic, minced
3 cups whole fresh mushrooms
4 medium carrots, cut into ¾-inch pieces
8 ounces pearl onions or 2 cups frozen small whole onions, thawed
3 tablespoons quick-cooking tapioca
1 teaspoon dried thyme, crushed
¾ teaspoon dried marjoram, crushed
½ teaspoon salt
¼ teaspoon pepper
2 bay leaves
1¼ cups Burgundy
½ cup beef broth
2 slices bacon, crisp-cooked, drained, and crumbled
3 cups hot cooked noodles

1 In a large skillet brown half of the meat in 1 tablespoon of the hot oil; remove meat from pan. Add remaining oil, remaining meat, chopped onion, and garlic. Cook until meat is brown and onion is tender. Drain off fat.

2 In a 3½- or 4-quart crockery cooker layer mushrooms, carrots, and pearl onions. Sprinkle with tapioca. Place meat mixture on top of vegetables. Add thyme, marjoram, salt, pepper, and bay leaves. Pour Burgundy and beef broth over meat and vegetables.

3 Cover and cook on low-heat setting for 10 to 12 hours or on high-heat setting for 5 to 6 hours or until tender. Remove and discard bay leaves. Stir in bacon and serve with noodles.

Nutrition Facts per serving: 446 cal., 19 g total fat (7 g sat. fat), 80 mg chol., 367 mg sodium, 39 g carbo., 4 g fiber, 22 g pro.
Daily Values: 104% vit. A, 12% vit. C, 6% calcium, 24% iron

Old-Fashioned Beef Stew

In the depths of winter, when temperatures plunge and darkness comes early, welcome your family home with steaming bowls of this perennial favorite.

Prep: 25 minutes   **Cook:** 10 to 12 hours   **Serves:** 4 to 6

2 tablespoons all-purpose flour
1 pound beef or pork stew meat, cut into ¾-inch cubes
2 tablespoons cooking oil
2½ cups cubed potatoes
1 cup frozen cut green beans*
1 cup frozen whole kernel corn*
1 cup sliced carrot
1 medium onion, cut into thin wedges
2 teaspoons instant beef bouillon granules
2 teaspoons Worcestershire sauce
1 teaspoon dried oregano, crushed
½ teaspoon dried marjoram or basil, crushed
¼ teaspoon pepper
1 bay leaf
2½ cups vegetable juice or hot-style vegetable juice

1 Place flour in a plastic bag. Add meat cubes and shake until meat is coated with flour. In a large skillet brown half of the meat in 1 tablespoon of the hot oil, turning to brown evenly. Brown remaining meat in remaining oil. Drain off fat.

2 In a 3½- or 4-quart crockery cooker layer potatoes, green beans, corn, carrot, and onion. Add meat. Add bouillon granules, Worcestershire sauce, oregano, marjoram, pepper, and bay leaf. Pour vegetable juice over all.

3 Cover and cook on low-heat setting for 10 to 12 hours or on high-heat setting for 5 to 6 hours or until meat and vegetables are tender. Discard bay leaf. Ladle into bowls.

Nutrition Facts per serving: 525 cal., 28 g total fat (10 g sat. fat), 77 mg chol., 953 mg sodium, 42 g carbo., 6 g fiber, 27 g pro.
Daily Values: 105% vit. A, 119% vit. C, 7% calcium, 29% iron

*Note: If you like, substitute 2 cups frozen mixed vegetables for the beans and corn.

For a 6-quart cooker: Recipe may be doubled.

Salsa Verde Beef Stew ♥

Mexican-style stewed tomatoes, salsa, and tortillas lend a south-of-the-border accent to this beef stew. Complete the meal with a festive salad of greens, orange sections, and avocado slices.

Prep: 30 minutes **Cook:** 8 to 9 hours **Serves:** 6

1½ pounds boneless beef
   chuck pot roast
1 tablespoon cooking oil
4 medium unpeeled Yukon
   Gold or other potatoes,
   cut into 1-inch pieces
1 large onion, coarsely
   chopped
1 green sweet pepper, cut
   into ½-inch pieces
1 14½-ounce can
   Mexican-style
   stewed tomatoes
1 15- or 16-ounce can pinto
   beans, rinsed and
   drained
1 cup bottled mild or
   medium green salsa
2 cloves garlic, minced
1 teaspoon ground cumin
6 flour tortillas, warmed

1 Trim fat from meat. Cut beef into 1-inch cubes. In a large skillet brown half of the beef at a time in hot oil over medium-high heat.

2 In a 3½- to 5-quart crockery cooker combine beef, potatoes, onion, sweet pepper, undrained tomatoes, beans, salsa, garlic, and cumin. Cover and cook on low-heat setting for 8 to 9 hours or on high-heat setting for 5 to 6 hours. Serve with warm tortillas.

Nutrition Facts per serving: 465 cal., 12 g total fat (3 g sat. fat), 72 mg chol., 709 mg sodium, 56 g carbo., 8 g fiber, 33 g pro.
Daily Values: 4% vit. A, 51% vit. C, 11% calcium, 31% iron

Zesty Beef Soup

Instant coffee crystals and a trio of spices—cumin, ginger, and allspice—lend a rich brown color and piquant flavor to this meaty vegetable soup.

Prep: 30 minutes **Cook:** 8 to 10 hours **Serves:** 6

2 tablespoons all-purpose flour

1 pound beef stew meat, cut into 1-inch cubes

2 tablespoons cooking oil

12 ounces tiny new potatoes, halved or quartered

4 medium carrots, cut into ½-inch pieces

1 large onion, chopped

1 cup beef broth

1 14½-ounce can chunky chili-style tomatoes or one 14½-ounce can diced tomatoes plus ½ to 1 teaspoon crushed red pepper

¾ cup water

2 tablespoons brown sugar

1 tablespoon Worcestershire sauce

1 tablespoon cider vinegar

1½ teaspoons instant coffee crystals

1 teaspoon ground cumin

½ teaspoon ground ginger

¼ teaspoon ground allspice

1 Place flour in a plastic bag. Add beef cubes and shake until beef is coated with flour. In a large skillet brown half of the meat in 1 tablespoon of the hot oil, turning to brown evenly. Remove beef from skillet. Brown remaining beef in remaining oil. Drain off fat.

2 In a 3½- or 4-quart crockery cooker place potatoes, carrots, and onion. Add meat.

3 In a bowl stir together beef broth, undrained tomatoes, water, brown sugar, Worcestershire sauce, vinegar, coffee crystals, cumin, ginger, and allspice. Pour over all.

4 Cover and cook on low-heat setting for 8 to 10 hours or on high-heat setting for 4 to 5 hours or until meat and vegetables are tender. Ladle into bowls.

Nutrition Facts per serving: 344 cal., 19 g total fat (7 g sat. fat), 53 mg chol., 551 mg sodium, 25 g carbo., 4 g fiber, 18 g pro.
Daily Values: 107% vit. A, 29% vit. C, 5% calcium, 16% iron

Sausage and Cabbage Soup

This full-flavored soup requires just a handful of ingredients. Packaged coleslaw mix keeps the prep time to a minimum because the cabbage is already shredded.

Prep: 15 minutes **Cook:** 10 to 12 hours **Serves:** 6

2 cups cubed peeled potatoes

4 cups packaged shredded cabbage with carrot (coleslaw mix)

1 large onion, chopped

2 teaspoons caraway seed, crushed

1 pound cooked Polish sausage, halved lengthwise and cut into ½-inch slices

4 cups reduced-sodium chicken broth

1 In a 3½- to 6-quart crockery cooker place potatoes, cabbage with carrot, onion, caraway seed, and sausage. Pour broth over all.

2 Cover and cook on low-heat setting for 10 to 12 hours or on high-heat setting for 5 to 6 hours. Ladle into bowls.

Nutrition Facts per serving: 322 cal., 22 g total fat (8 g sat. fat), 53 mg chol., 1,087 mg sodium, 16 g carbo., 3 g fiber, 15 g pro.
Daily Values: 1% vit. A, 42% vit. C, 5% calcium, 11% iron

broth options

Canned broths and bouillon granules and cubes are handy alternatives to homemade chicken, beef, or vegetable broth. Canned chicken, beef, and vegetable broth are ready to use straight from the can. Instant bouillon granules and cubes can be purchased in beef, chicken, vegetable, and onion flavors. One cube or 1 teaspoon of granules mixed with 1 cup boiling water makes an easy broth. If you are watching your sodium intake, use lower sodium broth and adjust the recipe's seasoning to taste.

Autumn Harvest Stew ♥

If you haven't thought of parsnips since you last read *The Tale of Peter Rabbit,* this nutty tasting root will be a treat. Look for parsnips that are firm with fairly smooth skin and few rootlets.

Prep: 25 minutes **Cook:** 7 to 8 hours **Serves:** 4

1 pound boneless pork
   shoulder
2 cups cubed, peeled sweet
   potatoes
2 medium parsnips, cut into
   ½-inch pieces
2 small cooking apples,
   cored and cut into
   ¼-inch slices
1 medium onion, chopped
¾ teaspoon dried thyme,
   crushed
½ teaspoon dried rosemary,
   crushed
½ teaspoon salt
¼ teaspoon pepper
2 cups apple cider or apple
   juice

1 Trim fat from meat. Cut meat into 1-inch cubes. In a 3½- or 4-quart crockery cooker layer potatoes, parsnips, apples, and onion. Sprinkle with thyme, rosemary, salt, and pepper. Add meat. Pour apple cider or juice over all.

2 Cover and cook on low-heat setting for 7 to 8 hours or on high-heat setting for 3½ to 4 hours or until meat and vegetables are tender. Ladle into bowls.

Nutrition Facts per serving: 365 cal., 8 g total fat (3 g sat. fat), 76 mg chol., 392 mg sodium, 37 g carbo., 7 g fiber, 24 g pro.
Daily Values: 121% vit. A, 40% vit. C, 7% calcium, 16% iron

Ham and Lentil Soup ♥

Unlike dry beans, lentils simmer to perfection in your crockery cooker without precooking. In this soup, lemon peel and spinach freshen the mild, nutty taste of the lentils.

Prep: 15 minutes **Cook:** 7 to 8 hours plus 10 minutes **Serves:** 4 to 6

1   cup dry lentils
4   cups water
1   medium onion, chopped
1   cup chopped celery
1   cup sliced carrot
2   teaspoons instant chicken
      bouillon granules
1   teaspoon bottled minced
      garlic or 2 cloves garlic,
      minced
½   teaspoon finely shredded
      lemon peel
⅛   to ¼ teaspoon ground red
      pepper
1   cup cubed cooked ham
2   cups chopped fresh
      spinach

1 Rinse and drain lentils. In a 3½- or 4-quart crockery cooker combine lentils, water, onion, celery, carrot, bouillon granules, garlic, lemon peel, and red pepper.

2 Cover and cook on low-heat setting for 7 to 8 hours or on high-heat setting for 3½ to 4 hours. If using low-heat setting, turn to high-heat setting. Add ham. Cover and cook for 10 minutes more on high-heat setting. Stir in chopped spinach; serve immediately.

Nutrition Facts per serving: 235 cal., 4 g total fat (1 g sat. fat), 21 mg chol., 815 mg sodium, 33 g carbo., 6 g fiber, 18 g pro.
Daily Values: 97% vit. A, 20% vit. C, 9% calcium, 27% iron

For a 5- to 6-quart cooker: Recipe may be doubled.

soup toppers

Keep soup and stew garnishes simple. I sprinkle soups with snipped fresh herbs or sliced green onions to give a snappy color. If I want to add a little crunch, I sprinkle them with croutons. A slice of lemon, a little grated cheese, a few chopped nuts, sieved cooked egg white or yolk, or shredded radishes complement the color and flavor of many soups.

Jennifer Kalinowski
Test Kitchen Home Economist

Tuscan Sausage and Bean Soup

Savor the flavors of sun-drenched Tuscany with this hearty vegetable soup. Serve with wedges of focaccia or thick slices of buttery garlic bread.

Prep: 20 minutes **Stand:** 1 hour **Cook:** 9 to 10 hours plus 10 minutes **Serves:** 6

1¼ cups dry Great Northern beans
4 cups cold water
8 ounces uncooked Italian sausage links, cut into ½- to ¾-inch slices
2¼ cups water
2 14½-ounce cans beef broth
1 large onion, chopped
2 cloves garlic, minced
1 teaspoon dried Italian seasoning, crushed
1 medium yellow summer squash or zucchini, sliced (about 1½ cups)
⅓ cup dry red wine or water
½ of a 10-ounce package frozen chopped spinach, thawed and well drained
1 14½-ounce can low-sodium diced tomatoes
Grated Parmesan cheese (optional)

1 Rinse dry beans. In a large saucepan combine beans and the 4 cups cold water. Bring to boiling; reduce heat. Simmer for 10 minutes. Remove from heat. Cover and let stand about 1 hour. Drain and rinse beans.

2 Meanwhile, in a medium skillet cook Italian sausage until brown. Drain well on paper towels.

3 In a 3½- to 5-quart crockery cooker combine the drained beans, the drained sausage, the 2¼ cups water, the beef broth, onion, garlic, Italian seasoning, summer squash or zucchini, and wine or water.

4 Cover and cook on low-heat setting for 9 to 10 hours or on high-heat setting for 5 to 6 hours or until beans are tender.

5 If using low-heat setting, turn to high-heat setting. Stir spinach and undrained tomatoes into soup. Cover and cook for 10 to 15 minutes more on high-heat setting or until heated through. Ladle into bowls. If desired, sprinkle with Parmesan cheese.

Nutrition Facts per serving: 329 cal., 14 g total fat (5 g sat. fat), 31 mg chol., 841 mg sodium, 33 g carbo., 10 g fiber, 17 g pro.
Daily Values: 41% vit. A, 20% vit. C, 12% calcium, 16% iron

Tex-Mex Chili

Fresh jalapeño peppers ignite the fire in this meaty chili. Douse the flames with glasses of ice-cold beer. For a milder version, omit the jalapeños and add a 4-ounce can of diced mild chili peppers.

Prep: 20 min **Cook:** 8 to 10 hours **Serves:** 4 to 6

1 pound bulk pork sausage or ground beef
1 15-ounce can red kidney beans, rinsed and drained
1 cup chopped celery
1 large onion, chopped
½ cup chopped green sweet pepper
1 to 2 fresh jalapeño peppers, seeded and chopped*
1 14½-ounce can tomatoes, cut up
1 10-ounce can chopped tomatoes and green chili peppers
1 cup hot-style vegetable juice or vegetable juice
1 6-ounce can low-sodium tomato paste
2 cloves garlic, minced
3 to 4 teaspoons chili powder
½ teaspoon ground cumin
½ cup shredded cheddar cheese (2 ounces)
¼ to ⅓ cup dairy sour cream

1 In a large skillet cook the sausage or beef until meat is brown. Drain off fat.

2 In a 3½- to 5-quart crockery cooker combine cooked meat, beans, celery, onion, sweet pepper, and jalapeño peppers. Add both cans of undrained tomatoes, vegetable juice, tomato paste, garlic, chili powder, and cumin.

3 Cover and cook on low-heat setting for 8 to 10 hours or on high-heat setting for 4 to 5 hours. Ladle chili into bowls. Pass cheese and sour cream with chili.

Nutrition Facts per serving: 665 cal., 41 g total fat (18 g sat. fat), 85 mg chol., 1,432 mg sodium, 44 g carbo., 12 g fiber, 30 g pro.
Daily Values: 43% vit. A, 115% vit. C, 27% calcium, 25% iron

***Note:** Hot peppers contain oils that can burn eyes, lips, and sensitive skin. Wear plastic gloves while preparing peppers and be sure to wash your hands thoroughly afterward.

Winter Minestrone

Any variety of winter squash—butternut, acorn, hubbard, or turban—will furnish this version of the classic Italian vegetable soup with a bright color and gentle sweetness.

Prep: 40 minutes **Cook:** 8 to 10 hours plus 5 minutes **Serves:** 8

1 pound uncooked Italian or pork sausage links, cut into ¾-inch slices
2½ cups peeled winter squash, such as butternut, acorn, hubbard, or turban, cut into 1-inch cubes
1½ cups peeled potatoes cut into 1-inch pieces
2 medium fennel bulbs, trimmed and cut into 1-inch pieces
1 large onion, chopped
2 cloves garlic, minced
1 15-ounce can red kidney beans, rinsed and drained
½ teaspoon dried sage, crushed
4 cups chicken broth or vegetable broth
1 cup dry white wine
4 cups chopped kale or fresh spinach

1 In a large skillet cook the sausage until brown; drain well. In a 5- to 6-quart crockery cooker place squash, potatoes, fennel, onion, garlic, beans, and sage. Top with sausage. Pour broth and wine over all.

2 Cover and cook on low-heat setting for 8 to 10 hours or on high-heat setting for 4 to 5 hours. Stir in kale or spinach. Cover and cook for 5 minutes more.

Nutrition Facts per serving: 315 cal., 14 g total fat (5 g sat. fat), 38 mg chol., 933 mg sodium, 27 g carbo., 14 g fiber, 16 g pro.
Daily Values: 61% vit. A, 69% vit. C, 11% calcium, 13% iron

Southern Ham Stew ♥

Dish up down-home cooking with this hearty stew featuring Southern standbys: collard greens, black-eyed peas, okra, and hominy.

Prep: 20 minutes **Cook:** 8 to 10 hours plus 10 minutes **Serves:** 8

1½ cups dry black-eyed peas (about 9½ ounces)

4 cups water

2 cups cubed cooked ham

1 15-ounce can white hominy, rinsed and drained

1 10-ounce package frozen cut okra

1 large onion, chopped

4 cloves garlic, minced

1 to 2 teaspoons Cajun or Creole seasoning or Homemade Cajun Seasoning (see recipe, page 60)

¼ teaspoon pepper

4½ cups water

4 cups chopped collard greens or fresh spinach

1 14½-ounce can stewed tomatoes

1 Rinse peas; drain. In a large saucepan combine peas and the 4 cups water. Bring to boiling; reduce heat. Simmer, uncovered, for 10 minutes. Drain and rinse peas.

2 In a 3½- to 6-quart crockery cooker combine peas, ham, hominy, frozen okra, onion, garlic, Cajun or Creole seasoning, and pepper. Stir in the 4½ cups fresh water.

3 Cover and cook on low-heat setting for 8 to 10 hours or on high-heat setting for 4 to 5 hours. If using low-heat setting, turn to high-heat setting. Stir in collard greens and undrained tomatoes. Cover and cook about 10 minutes more on high-heat setting or until heated through. Ladle into bowls.

Nutrition Facts per serving: 245 cal., 5 g total fat (1 g sat. fat), 20 mg chol., 673 mg sodium, 35 g carbo., 7 g fiber, 16 g pro.
Daily Values: 12% vit. A, 21% vit. C, 11% calcium, 21% iron

Potato and Leek Soup ♥

A package of frozen hash brown potatoes frees you from the tiresome task of peeling and chopping potatoes. Slice a loaf of pumpernickel bread to serve with this extra-easy, extra-creamy soup

Prep: 15 minutes **Cook:** 7 to 9 hours plus 10 minutes **Serves:** 10 to 12

3 cups water
1 1.8-ounce envelope white sauce mix
1 28-ounce package frozen loose-pack diced hash brown potatoes with onion and peppers
3 medium leeks, sliced (about 1 cup total)
1 cup finely chopped Canadian-style bacon or cooked ham
1 12-ounce can evaporated milk
½ teaspoon dried dillweed
1 8-ounce carton dairy sour cream
Snipped fresh parsley or sliced leek (optional)

1 In a 3½- or 4-quart crockery cooker gradually stir water into white sauce mix until mixture is smooth. Stir in frozen potatoes, the 3 leeks, Canadian-style bacon or ham, evaporated milk, and dillweed.

2 Cover and cook on low-heat setting for 7 to 9 hours or on high-heat setting for 3½ to 4½ hours.

3 If using low-heat setting, turn to high-heat setting. In a medium bowl stir about 2 cups of the hot potato mixture into the sour cream. Return sour cream mixture to cooker. Cover and cook about 10 minutes more on high-heat setting or until heated through. Ladle into bowls. If desired, sprinkle with parsley or additional sliced leek.

Nutrition Facts per serving: 212 cal., 10 g total fat (5 g sat. fat), 28 mg chol., 476 mg sodium, 23 g carbo., 1 g fiber, 8 g pro.
Daily Values: 6% vit. A, 14% vit. C, 13% calcium, 7% iron

advice for night owls

The early bird catches the worm, but if you're not a morning person, get a head start on your crockery cooker meal the night before. If the recipe calls for cooked meat or poultry, cook it the night before. You also can brown ground beef, ground poultry, or ground sausage. However, wait to brown meat cubes, poultry pieces, and roasts until the morning. Ground meats are completely cooked when browned and safe to refrigerate overnight, but larger cuts of meat are not cooked through after browning. Clean and chop vegetables. Store the prepared ingredients in separate containers in the refrigerator overnight. In the morning assemble the recipe, turn on the cooker, and be on your way.

Moroccan Lamb and Fruit Stew

A flavorful mix of spices teams up with dried apricots and dates to provide an exotic spicy-sweet taste. Serve the stew with couscous, a tiny pasta that's a staple in North African cuisine.

Prep: 30 minutes **Cook:** 7 to 9 hours plus 30 minutes **Serves:** 6 to 8

2 pounds boneless leg of lamb or beef bottom round roast

1 to 2 teaspoons crushed red pepper

¾ teaspoon ground turmeric

¾ teaspoon ground ginger

¾ teaspoon ground cinnamon

½ teaspoon salt

2 tablespoons olive oil or cooking oil

2 large onions, chopped

3 cloves garlic, minced

1 14½-ounce can beef broth

1 tablespoon cornstarch

2 tablespoons cold water

1 cup pitted dates

1 cup dried apricots
   Hot cooked couscous or rice

¼ cup toasted slivered almonds
   Orange peel curls (optional)

1 Trim fat from meat. Cut meat into 1- to 1½-inch cubes. In a shallow bowl combine the crushed red pepper, turmeric, ginger, cinnamon, and salt. Coat meat with the spice mixture. In a large skillet heat oil over medium-high heat. Brown the meat, one-third at a time, in the hot oil. Transfer meat to a 3½- or 4-quart crockery cooker. Add onions and garlic; stir to combine. Pour beef broth over all.

2 Cover and cook on low-heat setting for 7 to 9 hours or on high-heat setting for 3½ to 4½ hours or until meat is tender.

3 Skim off fat from cooking juices. In a small bowl combine cornstarch and cold water; stir into cooker. Add dates and apricots; stir to combine. If using low-heat setting, turn to high-heat setting. Cover and cook for 30 minutes more on high-heat setting or until mixture is slightly thickened and bubbly. To serve, spoon stew over hot couscous or rice. Top with almonds. If desired, garnish with orange peel curls.

Nutrition Facts per serving: 550 cal., 14 g total fat (3 g sat. fat), 76 mg chol., 475 mg sodium, 75 g carbo., 12 g fiber, 34 g pro.
Daily Values: 18% vit. A, 7% vit. C, 6% calcium, 29% iron

Asian Turkey and Rice Soup ♥

Slices of mushrooms, slivers of bok choy, and chunks of turkey mingle in a soy- and ginger-scented broth, giving stir-fry flavors to this savory soup.

Prep: 25 minutes **Cook:** 8 to 10 hours plus 5 minutes **Serves:** 6

2 cups sliced fresh mushrooms, such as shiitake or button

1½ cups sliced bok choy

1 medium onion, chopped

2 medium carrots, cut into bite-size strips (1 cup)

1 pound turkey breast tenderloins or skinless, boneless chicken breast halves, cut into 1-inch pieces

2 14½-ounce cans reduced-sodium chicken broth

2 tablespoons reduced-sodium soy sauce

1 tablespoon toasted sesame oil (optional)

4 cloves garlic, minced

2 teaspoons grated fresh ginger

1 cup instant rice

1 In a 3½- or 4-quart crockery cooker place mushrooms, bok choy, onion, and carrots. Add turkey or chicken to cooker. Combine chicken broth, soy sauce, sesame oil (if desired), garlic, and ginger. Pour over vegetables and turkey.

2 Cover and cook on low-heat setting for 8 to 10 hours or on high-heat setting for 4 to 5 hours. Stir in rice. Cover and cook for 5 to 10 minutes or until rice is tender. Ladle into bowls.

Nutrition Facts per serving: 186 cal., 1 g total fat (0 g sat. fat), 47 mg chol., 584 mg sodium, 20 g carbo., 1 g fiber, 24 g pro.
Daily Values: 62% vit. A, 19% vit. C, 4% calcium, 11% iron

For a 5- to 6-quart cooker: Recipe may be doubled.

Brunswick Stew ♥

Early Virginia settlers made this hearty stew with squirrel meat. Our updated version simmers all day in your crockery cooker and features chicken and smoked pork hocks.

Prep: 20 minutes **Cook:** 8 to 10 hours plus 30 minutes **Serves:** 4 or 5

2 pounds meaty chicken
   pieces, skinned
1½ cups chopped cooked ham
3 medium onions, cut into
   thin wedges
1 14½-ounce can diced
   tomatoes
½ cup chicken broth
4 cloves garlic, minced
1 tablespoon Worcestershire
   sauce
1 teaspoon dry mustard
1 teaspoon dried thyme,
   crushed
¼ teaspoon pepper
¼ teaspoon bottled hot
   pepper sauce
1 10-ounce package frozen
   whole or sliced okra
1 cup frozen baby lima
   beans
1 cup frozen whole kernel
   corn

1 In a 3½- to 6-quart crockery cooker place chicken, ham, and onions. Add undrained tomatoes, broth, garlic, Worcestershire sauce, mustard, thyme, pepper, and hot pepper sauce.

2 Cover and cook on low-heat setting for 8 to 10 hours or on high-heat setting for 4 to 5 hours.

3 Remove chicken; cool slightly. Remove meat from bones. Cut meat into bite-size pieces; discard bones. Return chicken to crockery cooker.

4 Add okra, lima beans, and corn to crockery cooker. If using low-heat setting, turn to high-heat setting. Cover and cook 30 minutes more or until vegetables are tender.

Nutrition Facts per serving: 417 cal., 11 g total fat (3 g sat. fat), 124 mg chol., 1,252 mg sodium, 36 g carbo., 7 g fiber, 43 g pro.
Daily Values: 17% vit. A, 65% vit. C, 15% calcium, 26% iron

Indian Vegetable Soup ♥

Chock-full of nutty tasting garbanzo beans, red potatoes, and chunks of eggplant, this curried soup can double as a meatless entrée or a substantial side dish.

Prep: 30 minutes **Cook:** 8 to 10 hours **Serves:** 6 to 8

1 medium eggplant, cut into ½-inch cubes (5 to 6 cups)
1 pound red potatoes, cut into 1-inch pieces (3 cups)
2 cups chopped tomatoes or one 14½-ounce can low-sodium tomatoes, cut up
1 15-ounce can garbanzo beans, rinsed and drained
1 tablespoon grated fresh ginger
1½ teaspoons mustard seed
1½ teaspoons ground coriander
1 teaspoon curry powder
¼ teaspoon pepper
4 cups vegetable broth or chicken broth
2 tablespoons snipped cilantro

1 In a 4- to 6-quart crockery cooker combine eggplant, potatoes, undrained tomatoes, and garbanzo beans.

2 Sprinkle the ginger, mustard seed, coriander, curry powder, and pepper over vegetables. Pour vegetable broth or chicken broth over all.

3 Cover and cook on low-heat setting for 8 to 10 hours or on high-heat setting for 4 to 5 hours. Ladle into bowls and sprinkle with cilantro.

Nutrition Facts per serving: 162 cal., 2 g total fat (0 g sat. fat), 0 mg chol., 889 mg sodium, 30 g carbo., 7 g fiber, 8 g pro.
Daily Values: 7% vit. A, 33% vit. C, 4% calcium, 10% iron

Fennel-Barley Soup ♥

Looking for a soup and sandwich supper? Pair this full-flavored soup with your family's favorite sandwiches, such as grilled cheese, tuna salad, or submarines.

Prep: 25 minutes **Cook:** 8 to 10 hours **Serves:** 8

  2 medium fennel bulbs,
       trimmed and chopped
       (2 cups)
  2 medium zucchini,
       chopped (2½ cups)
  1 large onion, chopped
  ½ cup regular barley
  2 cloves garlic, minced
  1 tablespoon snipped leafy
       tops of fennel
  ¼ teaspoon pepper
  4 cups reduced-sodium
       vegetable juice or
       hot-style vegetable juice
  2 cups water
  1 14½-ounce can vegetable
       broth or chicken broth

1 In a 3½- or 4-quart crockery cooker combine fennel, zucchini, onion, barley, garlic, fennel tops, and pepper. Stir in vegetable juice, water, and broth.

2 Cover and cook on low-heat setting for 8 to 10 hours or on high-heat setting for 4 to 5 hours.

Nutrition Facts per serving: 95 cal., 1 g total fat (0 g sat. fat), 0 mg chol., 296 mg sodium, 21 g carbo., 9 g fiber, 3 g pro.
Daily Values: 27% vit. A, 62% vit. C, 5% calcium, 7% iron

cutting vegetables to size

Vegetables intended for the crockery cooker are cut into bite-size pieces for easier eating as well as better cooking. In crockery cookers, some vegetables take longer to cook than meat. By cutting vegetables into small pieces (and, if using large pieces of meat, placing the meat on top of the vegetables), you can be sure the vegetables will be tender and ready to eat when the meat is done.

Southwestern Bean Soup ♥

Fluffy cornmeal dumplings top bowls of this zippy bean soup. To ensure proper cooking, don't lift the lid until you're ready to test dumplings for doneness.

Prep: 25 minutes **Cook:** 10 to 12 hours plus 30 minutes **Serves:** 6

3 cups water
1 15-ounce can red kidney beans, rinsed and drained
1 15-ounce can black beans, pinto beans, or Great Northern beans, rinsed and drained
1 14½-ounce can Mexican-style stewed tomatoes
1 10-ounce package frozen whole kernel corn
1 cup sliced carrot
1 large onion, chopped
1 4-ounce can diced green chili peppers
2 tablespoons instant beef or chicken bouillon granules
1 to 2 teaspoons chili powder
2 cloves garlic, minced
⅓ cup all-purpose flour
¼ cup yellow cornmeal
1 teaspoon baking powder
  Dash pepper
1 beaten egg white
2 tablespoons milk
1 tablespoon cooking oil

1 In a 3½- or 4-quart crockery cooker combine water, beans, undrained tomatoes, corn, carrot, onion, undrained chili peppers, bouillon granules, chili powder, and garlic.

2 Cover and cook on low-heat setting for 10 to 12 hours or on high-heat setting for 5 to 6 hours.

3 For dumplings, in a medium mixing bowl stir together flour, cornmeal, baking powder, and pepper. In a small mixing bowl combine egg white, milk, and oil. Add to flour mixture; stir with a fork just until combined.

4 Drop dumpling mixture in 6 mounds on top of the bubbling soup. Cover and cook on low-heat setting for 30 minutes more or on high-heat setting for 20 minutes more or until a wooden toothpick inserted in center of dumpling comes out clean. Do not lift lid while dumplings are cooking. Ladle into bowls and top each serving with a dumpling.

Nutrition Facts per serving: 263 cal., 4 g total fat (1 g sat. fat), 1 mg chol., 1,434 mg sodium, 51 g carbo., 11 g fiber, 15 g pro.
Daily Values: 56% vit. A, 17% vit. C, 15% calcium, 15% iron

Italian Bean Soup ♥

Float thick slices of buttered garlic toast on this hearty meat-free soup. Three kinds of beans—Great Northern, red, and Italian-style green—provide plenty of protein and vitamins.

Prep: 15 minutes **Stand:** 1 hour **Cook:** 11 to 13 hours plus 30 minutes **Serves:** 6

1 cup dry Great Northern beans
1 cup dry red beans or pinto beans
4 cups water
1 medium onion, chopped
2 tablespoons instant beef bouillon granules
2 cloves garlic, minced
2 teaspoons dried Italian seasoning, crushed
¼ teaspoon pepper
1 28-ounce can tomatoes, cut-up
1 9-ounce package frozen Italian green beans or cut green beans, thawed
2 tablespoons margarine or butter
¼ teaspoon garlic powder
¼ teaspoon dried Italian seasoning, crushed
12 ½-inch-thick slices baguette-style French bread

1 Rinse dry beans. In a Dutch oven combine rinsed beans and 5 cups cold water. Bring to boiling; reduce heat. Simmer for 10 minutes. Remove from heat. Cover and let stand about 1 hour. Drain and rinse beans.

2 In a 3½- to 6-quart crockery cooker combine beans, the 4 cups fresh water, onion, bouillon granules, garlic, the 2 teaspoons Italian seasoning, and the pepper.

3 Cover and cook on low-heat setting for 11 to 13 hours or on high-heat setting for 5½ to 6½ hours or until beans are almost tender. If using low-heat setting, turn to high-heat setting. Stir undrained tomatoes and thawed green beans into soup. Cover and cook about 30 minutes more on high-heat setting or until beans are tender.

4 Meanwhile, stir together margarine or butter, garlic powder, and the ¼ teaspoon Italian seasoning. Spread on 1 side of each bread slice. Place bread, margarine side up, on the unheated rack of a broiler pan. Broil 4 to 5 inches from the heat for 1 to 2 minutes or until crisp and light brown. To serve, ladle soup into bowls. Float 2 pieces of herb toast on each serving. Serve immediately.

Nutrition Facts per serving: 432 cal., 6 g total fat (1 g sat. fat), 0 mg chol., 1,619 mg sodium, 75 g carbo., 15 g fiber, 20 g pro.
Daily Values: 13% vit. A, 29% vit. C, 15% calcium, 30% iron

Meats

Pork Chops with
Orange Sauce

In This Chapter:

Beef Pot Roast

With a crockery cooker you can fix this perennial favorite any day of the week. Stop by the bakery, pick up an apple pie for dessert, and treat your family to an all-American dinner.

Prep: 30 minutes **Cook:** 10 to 12 hours **Serves:** 6 to 8

1 2- to 2½-pound boneless beef chuck pot roast
1 tablespoon cooking oil
1 pound whole tiny new potatoes, 3 medium potatoes, or 3 medium sweet potatoes
8 carrots or parsnips, cut into 1-inch pieces
3 small onions, cut into wedges
¾ cup water
1 tablespoon Worcestershire sauce
2 teaspoons instant beef bouillon granules
1 teaspoon dried basil or oregano, crushed
½ cup cold water
¼ cup all-purpose flour

1 Trim fat from roast. If necessary, cut roast to fit into a 3½- or 4-quart crockery cooker. In a large skillet brown meat on all sides in hot oil. Drain off fat.

2 Meanwhile, remove a narrow strip of peel from the center of each new potato, or peel and quarter each medium potato or sweet potato. Place potatoes, carrots or parsnips, and onions in cooker. Place meat on top of vegetables.

3 In a small bowl combine the ¾ cup water, Worcestershire sauce, bouillon granules, and basil or oregano. Pour over meat and vegetables.

4 Cover and cook on low-heat setting for 10 to 12 hours or on high-heat setting for 5 to 6 hours.

5 Transfer meat and vegetables to a serving platter, reserving juices; cover meat and keep warm. Pour cooking juices into a glass measuring cup; skim off fat. For gravy, measure 1½ cups juices, adding water if necessary. Transfer to a saucepan. In a small bowl combine the ½ cup cold water and flour; stir into juices in saucepan. Cook and stir until thickened and bubbly. Cook and stir for 1 minute more. Season gravy to taste with salt and pepper. Serve gravy with meat and vegetables.

Nutrition Facts per serving: 470 cal., 26 g total fat (9 g sat. fat), 98 mg chol., 426 mg sodium, 27 g carbo., 4 g fiber, 32 g pro.
Daily Values: 206% vit. A, 30% vit. C, 5% calcium, 26% iron

For a 5- to 6-quart cooker: Use a 3- to 3½-pound boneless beef chuck pot roast, cut in half; 1½ pounds potatoes; 10 carrots or parsnips; and 4 onions. Use remaining ingredients as directed above, except reserve 2½ cups juices (adding water, if necessary) for gravy. To thicken the gravy, combine ⅓ cup all-purpose flour with the ½ cup cold water. Makes 10 servings.

Dilled Pot Roast ♥

Kosher salt is more coarsely ground than regular table salt and contains no additives. Some cooks prefer the taste and texture of kosher salt for seasoning meat.

Prep: 20 minutes **Cook:** 10 to 12 hours **Serves:** 6 to 8

1 2- to 2½-pound boneless beef chuck pot roast
2 tablespoons cooking oil
½ cup water
1 teaspoon dried dillweed
1 teaspoon coarse salt (kosher) or ¾ teaspoon regular salt
½ teaspoon pepper
½ cup plain yogurt
2 tablespoons all-purpose flour
3 cups hot cooked noodles

1 If necessary, cut roast to fit into a 3½- or 4-quart crockery cooker. In a large skillet brown roast on all sides in hot oil. Transfer roast to cooker. Add the water to cooker. Sprinkle roast with ¾ teaspoon dillweed, salt, and pepper.

2 Cover and cook on low-heat setting for 10 to 12 hours or on high-heat setting for 5 to 6 hours or until meat is tender. Transfer roast to a serving platter, reserving juices; cover roast and keep warm. Pour cooking juices into a glass measuring cup; skim off fat. Measure 1 cup of the reserved juices.

3 For sauce, in a small saucepan stir together yogurt and flour until combined. Stir in the 1 cup reserved cooking juices and remaining dillweed. Cook and stir until thickened and bubbly. Cook and stir for 1 minute more. Serve with meat and noodles.

Nutrition Facts per serving: 373 cal., 12 g total fat (4 g sat. fat), 136 mg chol., 443 mg sodium, 22 g carbo., 2 g fiber, 41 g pro.
Daily Values: 0% vit. A, 0% vit. C, 4% calcium, 33% iron

Asian-Style Pot Roast ♥

Black bean garlic sauce, a staple in Chinese cuisine, gives a rich, exotic flavor to pot roast. Look for the bean sauce in the Asian foods section of the supermarket or in Asian grocery stores.

Prep: 30 minutes **Cook:** 10 to 12 hours plus 15 minutes **Serves:** 6

1   2-pound boneless beef
    chuck pot roast
1   tablespoon cooking oil
1½   cups hot water
¼   cup black bean garlic
    sauce
1   teaspoon instant beef
    bouillon granules
1   tablespoon sugar
1   medium red sweet pepper,
    cut into thin strips
½   medium white onion,
    sliced into thin strips
8   ounces green beans,
    trimmed
3   tablespoons cornstarch
3   tablespoons cold water
3   cups hot cooked white or
    brown rice

1 Trim fat from roast. If necessary, cut roast to fit into a 4- to 5½-quart crockery cooker. In a large skillet brown roast on all sides in hot oil. Drain off fat.

2 In the cooker stir together the 1½ cups water, bean sauce, bouillon granules, and sugar. Add sweet pepper, onion, and green beans. Place meat on top of vegetables.

3 Cover and cook on low-heat setting for 10 to 12 hours or on high-heat setting for 5 to 6 hours or until beef is tender.

4 Transfer meat and vegetables to a serving platter, reserving juices; cover meat and keep warm. If using low-heat setting, turn to high-heat setting. For sauce, in a small bowl combine cornstarch and cold water; stir into cooking juices in cooker. Cover and cook about 15 minutes more on high-heat setting or until sauce is slightly thickened.

5 Using two forks, separate beef into serving pieces. Serve meat over rice with the sauce and vegetables.

Nutrition Facts per serving: 382 cal., 11 g total fat (3 g sat. fat), 79 mg chol., 513 mg sodium, 34 g carbo., 3 g fiber, 35 g pro.
Daily Values: 13% vit. A, 64% vit. C, 6% calcium, 28% iron

Country Swiss Steak

The addition of spicy bratwurst brings a new flavor dimension to this American classic. To complete the hearty meal, warm crusty rolls in the oven and toss a salad.

Prep: 15 minutes **Cook:** 10 to 12 hours **Serves:** 4

1 pound boneless beef round steak, cut ¾ to 1 inch thick

4 ounces uncooked spicy bratwurst or other sausage, cut into ¾-inch slices

1 tablespoon cooking oil

1 small onion, sliced and separated into rings

2 tablespoons quick-cooking tapioca

1 teaspoon dried thyme, crushed

¼ teaspoon salt

¼ teaspoon pepper

1 14½-ounce can chunky tomatoes with garlic and spices

2 cups hot cooked noodles or rice

Fresh thyme sprigs (optional)

1 Trim fat from meat. Cut meat into 4 serving-size pieces. In a large skillet brown meat and bratwurst or sausage on all sides in hot oil. Drain off fat.

2 In a 3½- or 4-quart crockery cooker place onion. Sprinkle with tapioca, thyme, salt, and pepper. Pour undrained tomatoes over onion. Add meat.

3 Cover and cook on low-heat setting for 10 to 12 hours. Serve with noodles or rice. If desired, garnish with fresh thyme.

Nutrition Facts per serving: 531 cal., 28 g total fat (9 g sat. fat), 114 mg chol., 958 mg sodium, 37 g carbo., 4 g fiber, 32 g pro.
Daily Values: 12% vit. A, 21% vit. C, 6% calcium, 26% iron

Ginger Beef with Broccoli ♥

Brimming with all the flavors and fixings of a traditional stir fry, this ever-so-easy beef and veggie combo is draped in a sauce made with an envelope of gravy mix.

Prep: 20 minutes **Cook:** 8 to 10 hours plus 15 minutes **Serves:** 6

6 medium carrots, cut into 1-inch pieces
2 medium onions, cut into wedges
1½ pounds beef round steak, cut into ½-inch bias-sliced strips
1 tablespoon minced fresh ginger
2 cloves garlic, minced
½ cup water
2 tablespoons reduced-sodium soy sauce
1 ¾-ounce envelope beef gravy mix
4 cups broccoli flowerets
3 cups hot cooked rice

1 In a 3½- or 4-quart crockery cooker place carrots, onions, beef strips, ginger, and garlic. Stir together water, soy sauce, and beef gravy mix. Pour over meat and vegetables in cooker.

2 Cover and cook on low-heat setting for 8 to 10 hours or on high-heat setting for 4 to 5 hours.

3 If using low-heat setting, turn to high-heat setting. Stir in broccoli flowerets. Cover and cook about 15 minutes more on high-heat setting or until the broccoli is crisp-tender. Serve over hot cooked rice.

Nutrition Facts per serving: 327 cal., 6 g total fat (2 g sat. fat), 54 mg chol., 476 mg sodium, 37 g carbo., 4 g fiber, 31 g pro.
Daily Values: 163% vit. A, 88% vit. C, 8% calcium, 22% iron

toting foods safely

Foods prepared in crockery cookers are great for taking to picnics or parties. To tote, after the food is completely cooked, wrap the cooker in heavy foil, several layers of newspaper, or a thick towel. Place the cooker in an insulated container. The food should stay hot for up to 2 hours. (Do not hold the food for longer than 2 hours before serving). If there is electricity at your picnic or party site, plug in the cooker. The food will stay warm for hours on the low-heat setting.

Barbecued Beef Sandwiches

Beef brisket requires slow cooking in liquid, making it an excellent choice for crockery cooking. Slice brisket across the grain for fork-tender sandwiches.

Prep: 25 minutes **Cook:** 10 hours plus 10 to 20 minutes **Serves:** 10 to 12

1 2½- to 3-pound fresh beef brisket
1 10-ounce can chopped tomatoes and green chili peppers
1 8-ounce can (about 1 cup) applesauce
½ of a 6-ounce can (⅓ cup) tomato paste
¼ cup soy sauce
¼ cup packed brown sugar
1 tablespoon Worcestershire sauce
10 to 12 hamburger buns, split and toasted
   Sliced red onion (optional)
   Dill pickle slices (optional)

1 Trim fat from meat. If necessary, cut meat to fit into a 3½- or 4-quart crockery cooker. Place meat in cooker. In a bowl stir together the undrained tomatoes, applesauce, tomato paste, soy sauce, brown sugar, and Worcestershire sauce; pour over meat.

2 Cover and cook on low-heat setting 10 hours or on high-heat setting 5 hours or until meat is tender. Transfer meat to a carving board; reserve juices. Cover meat and keep warm.

3 Pour cooking juices into a medium saucepan. Skim off fat. Bring juices to boiling; reduce heat. Boil gently, uncovered, for 10 to 20 minutes or until reduced to desired consistency, stirring frequently. Thinly slice meat across the grain. Place meat on bun bottoms; drizzle with cooking juices. If desired, top with onion slices and pickles. Add bun tops.

Nutrition Facts per serving: 332 cal., 9 g total fat (3 g sat. fat), 54 mg chol., 836 mg sodium, 33 g carbo., 2 g fiber, 29 g pro.
Daily Values: 3% vit. A, 7% vit. C, 8% calcium, 22% iron

Sloppy Joes ♥

These kid-pleasing saucy sandwiches make perfect fare for birthday parties and family-style potlucks. The recipe makes a bunch and cooks with little attention.

Prep: 25 minutes **Cook:** 6 to 8 hours **Serves:** 16 to 20

2½ pounds ground beef
1 medium onion, chopped
3 cloves garlic, minced
1¼ cups catsup
1 medium green sweet
    pepper, chopped
2 stalks celery, chopped
⅓ cup water
3 tablespoons brown sugar
3 tablespoons prepared
    mustard
3 tablespoons vinegar
3 tablespoons
    Worcestershire sauce
1 tablespoon chili powder
16 to 20 hamburger buns,
    split and toasted

1 In a large skillet cook ground beef, onion, and garlic until meat is brown and onion is tender. Drain off fat.

2 In a 3½- or 4-quart crockery cooker combine catsup, sweet pepper, celery, water, brown sugar, mustard, vinegar, Worcestershire sauce, and chili powder. Stir in meat mixture.

3 Cover and cook on low-heat setting for 6 to 8 hours or on high-heat setting for 3 to 4 hours. Spoon into toasted buns.

Nutrition Facts per serving: 298 cal., 12 g total fat (4 g sat. fat), 44 mg chol., 579 mg sodium, 31 g carbo., 2 g fiber, 17 g pro.
Daily Values: 4% vit. A, 17% vit. C, 8% calcium, 17% iron

Apple Pork Roast and Vegetables

Savory and just slightly sweet from frozen apple juice concentrate, this pork pot roast makes a weeknight supper that your family will love.

Prep: 25 minutes **Cook:** 10 to 12 hours **Serves:** 6 to 8

1 2- to 2½-pound boneless
    pork shoulder roast
3 medium parsnips, cut into
    1-inch pieces (2 cups)
3 medium carrots, cut into
    1-inch pieces (1½ cups)
1 large green sweet pepper,
    cut lengthwise into
    1-inch wide strips
2 stalks celery, cut into
    1-inch pieces (1 cup)
3 tablespoons quick-cooking
    tapioca
1 6-ounce can (⅔ cup)
    frozen apple juice
    concentrate, thawed
¼ cup water
1 teaspoon instant beef
    bouillon granules
¼ teaspoon pepper

1 Trim fat from roast. In a 3½- or 4-quart crockery cooker place parsnips, carrots, sweet pepper, and celery. Sprinkle vegetables with tapioca. Add juice concentrate, water, bouillon granules, and pepper to cooker. Place roast on top of vegetables.

2 Cover and cook on low-heat setting for 10 to 12 hours or on high-heat setting for 5 to 6 hours.

3 To serve, transfer the meat and vegetables to a serving platter. Strain cooking juices; skim off fat. Drizzle some of the juices over the sliced meat and pass the remaining juices.

Nutrition Facts per serving: 269 cal., 7 g total fat (2 g sat. fat), 61 mg chol.,
250 mg sodium, 33 g carbo., 4 g fiber, 19 g pro.
Daily Values: 79% vit. A, 49% vit. C, 5% calcium, 11% iron

Pineapple-Ginger Pork ♥

Easier than stir fry, this colorful dish is destined to become a mainstay in your repertoire of fuss-free weeknight dinners.

Prep: 30 minutes **Cook:** 6 to 8 hours plus 10 to 15 minutes   **Serves:** 6 to 8

 2 pounds boneless pork
 shoulder
 2 tablespoons cooking oil
 ¾ cup chicken broth
 3 tablespoons quick-cooking
 tapioca
 3 tablespoons low-sodium
 soy sauce
 3 tablespoons oyster sauce
 (optional)
 1 teaspoon grated fresh
 ginger
 1 15¼-ounce can pineapple
 chunks (juice pack)
 4 medium carrots, cut into
 ½-inch slices (2 cups)
 1 large onion, cut into
 1-inch pieces
 1 8-ounce can sliced water
 chestnuts, drained
 1½ cups fresh snow pea pods
 or one 6-ounce package
 frozen pea pods
 3 cups hot cooked rice

1 Trim fat from pork. Cut pork into 1-inch cubes. In a large skillet brown half of the pork at a time in hot oil. Drain fat.

2 In a 3½- or 4-quart crockery cooker combine chicken broth, tapioca, soy sauce, oyster sauce (if using), and ginger. Drain pineapple, reserving juice. Stir juice into broth mixture; cover and chill pineapple chunks. Add carrots, onion, and water chestnuts to cooker. Add pork.

3 Cover and cook on low-heat setting for 6 to 8 hours or on high-heat setting for 3 to 4 hours.

4 If using low-heat setting, turn to high-heat setting. Stir pineapple chunks and the fresh or frozen snow peas into cooker. Cover and cook for 10 to 15 minutes more on high-heat setting or until peas are crisp-tender. Serve over rice.

Nutrition Facts per serving: 402 cal., 11 g total fat (3 g sat. fat), 62 mg chol., 477 mg sodium, 51 g carbo., 5 g fiber, 23 g pro.
Daily Values: 104% vit. A, 33% vit. C, 7% calcium, 17% iron

For a 5- to 6-quart cooker: Recipe may be doubled.

Lemon Pork and Couscous

Company coming in the middle of the week? No problem: Fix this easy combo of pork, carrots, and parsnips flavored with shallots, lemon, and fresh basil.

Prep: 30 minutes **Cook:** 7 to 8 hours plus 5 minutes **Serves:** 6

 2 pounds boneless pork
   shoulder
¼ cup all-purpose flour
½ teaspoon pepper
 2 tablespoons cooking oil
 1 16-ounce package peeled
   baby carrots
 8 ounces parsnips, cut into
   ½-inch slices
 2 medium shallots, sliced
 1 lemon, quartered
¼ cup thinly sliced fresh
   basil
 1 14½-ounce can chicken
   broth
1⅓ cups quick-cooking
   couscous

1 Trim fat from pork. Cut pork into 1-inch pieces. Combine flour and pepper in a plastic bag. Add pork, close bag, and shake until pork is coated. In a large skillet brown half of the meat in 1 tablespoon of the oil about 5 minutes, turning to brown evenly. Remove from skillet. Brown remaining pork in remaining 1 tablespoon oil about 5 minutes, turning to brown evenly.

2 In a 3½- to 6-quart crockery cooker place carrots, parsnips, shallots, lemon, and basil. Place pork on top of vegetables. Pour broth over all.

3 Cover and cook on low-heat setting for 7 to 8 hours or on high-heat setting for 3½ to 4 hours. Discard lemon pieces.

4 Use a slotted spoon to remove pork and vegetables to a serving dish, reserving juices; cover meat and keep warm. Measure 1¾ cups of the cooking juices and return to crockery cooker. Discard remaining cooking liquid. If using low-heat setting, turn to high-heat setting. Stir in couscous. Cover and cook for 5 minutes more on high-heat setting. Fluff couscous with a fork. Serve pork and vegetables over couscous.

Nutrition Facts per serving: 511 cal., 16 g total fat (4 g sat. fat), 101 mg chol., 368 mg sodium, 53 g carbo., 7 g fiber, 38 g pro.
Daily Values: 193% vit. A, 44% vit. C, 8% calcium, 20% iron

Pork and Lentil Cassoulet ♥

Lentils are a quick substitute for traditional beans in this classic French dish. They can be added to the crockery cooker straight from the package without precooking.

Prep: 20 minutes **Cook:** 10 to 12 hours **Serves:** 4

12 ounces boneless pork shoulder

1 large onion, cut into wedges

2 cloves garlic, minced

2 teaspoons cooking oil

2½ cups water

1 14½-ounce can tomatoes, cut up

4 medium carrots and/or parsnips, cut into ½-inch slices

2 stalks celery, thinly sliced

¾ cup dry lentils, rinsed and drained

1½ teaspoons dried rosemary, crushed

1 teaspoon instant beef bouillon granules

¼ teaspoon salt

¼ teaspoon pepper
Fresh rosemary sprigs (optional)

1 Trim fat from pork. Cut meat into ¾-inch cubes. In a large skillet brown pork, onion, and garlic in hot oil. Transfer mixture to a 3½- or 4-quart crockery cooker. Add the water, undrained tomatoes, carrots and/or parsnips, celery, lentils, rosemary, bouillon granules, salt, and pepper.

2 Cover and cook on low-heat setting for 10 to 12 hours or on high-heat setting for 4½ to 5½ hours. Ladle into bowls. If desired, garnish with fresh rosemary.

Nutrition Facts per serving: 354 cal., 12 g total fat (3 g sat. fat), 37 mg chol., 641 mg sodium, 37 g carbo., 5 g fiber, 26 g pro.
Daily Values: 167% vit. A, 37% vit. C, 8% calcium, 37% iron

Pulled Pork with Root Beer Sauce

Root beer gives these pork sandwiches a rich color and pleasant sweetness. Root beer concentrate intensifies the flavor. You'll find it in the spice section of your supermarket.

Prep: 15 minutes **Cook:** 8 to 10 hours **Serves:** 8 to 10

1 2½- to 3-pound pork
    sirloin roast
½ teaspoon salt
½ teaspoon pepper
1 tablespoon cooking oil
2 medium onions, cut into
    thin wedges
1 cup root beer*
2 tablespoons minced garlic
3 cups root beer (two
    12-ounce cans or
    bottles)*
1 cup bottled chili sauce
¼ teaspoon root beer
    concentrate (optional)
    Several dashes bottled hot
    pepper sauce (optional)
8 to 10 hamburger buns,
    split and toasted
    Lettuce leaves (optional)
    Tomato slices (optional)

1 Trim fat from meat. If necessary, cut roast to fit into a 3½- to 5-quart crockery cooker. Sprinkle the roast with salt and pepper. In a large skillet brown meat on all sides in hot oil. Drain off fat. Place meat in the crockery cooker. Add onions, the 1 cup root beer, and garlic.

2 Cover and cook on low-heat setting for 8 to 10 hours or on high-heat setting for 4 to 5 hours.

3 Meanwhile, for sauce, in a medium saucepan combine the 2 cans or bottles of root beer and the chili sauce. Bring to boiling; reduce heat. Boil gently, uncovered, stirring occasionally, about 30 minutes or until reduced to 2 cups. If desired, stir in root beer concentrate and bottled hot pepper sauce.

4 Transfer roast to a cutting board or serving platter. Using a slotted spoon, remove onions from cooking juices and place on serving platter. Discard juices. Using 2 forks, pull meat apart into shreds. If desired, line buns with lettuce leaves and tomato slices. Add meat and onions; spoon on sauce.

Nutrition Facts per serving: 356 cal., 10 g total fat (3 g sat. fat), 59 mg chol., 786 mg sodium, 44 g carbo., 1 g fiber, 22 g pro.
Daily Values: 4% vit. A, 9% vit. C, 4% calcium, 13% iron

*Note: Do not use diet root beer.

Ribs with Apples and Sauerkraut

Celebrate Oktoberfest any time of the year with this pork and sauerkraut supper. Round out the meal with rye rolls and ice-cold beer.

Prep: 30 minutes **Cook:** 8 to 10 hours plus 10 minutes **Serves:** 4

2½ pounds country-style pork ribs, cut crosswise in half and cut into 1- to 2-rib portions
1 tablespoon cooking oil
2 medium potatoes, cut into ½-inch slices
2 medium carrots, cut into ¼-inch slices
1 medium onion, thinly sliced
1 8-ounce can sauerkraut, rinsed and drained
½ cup apple cider or apple juice
2 teaspoons caraway or fennel seed
⅛ teaspoon ground cloves
2 tablespoons cold water
1 tablespoon all-purpose flour
½ of a large apple, cored and thinly sliced
1 tablespoon snipped parsley

1 In a large skillet brown pork ribs on both sides in hot oil over medium-high heat. In a 3½- or 4-quart crockery cooker place potatoes, carrots, and onion. Add browned pork ribs and sauerkraut. In a bowl combine apple cider or juice, caraway or fennel seed, and cloves. Pour over sauerkraut.

2 Cover and cook on low-heat setting for 8 to 10 hours or on high-heat setting for 4 to 5 hours. Transfer meat and vegetables to a serving platter, reserving juices; cover meat and keep warm.

3 For gravy, strain cooking juices into a glass measuring cup. Skim off fat. Measure 1 cup juices, adding water if necessary. Pour into a saucepan. In a small bowl, combine cold water and flour until smooth; stir into the juices in saucepan. Cook and stir over medium heat until thickened and bubbly. Stir in the apple. Cook and stir for 1 minute more or until heated through. If desired, season to taste with salt and pepper. Stir in parsley just before serving. Serve ribs with vegetables and gravy.

Nutrition Facts per serving: 431 cal., 20 g total fat (7 g sat. fat), 103 mg chol., 371 mg sodium, 32 g carbo., 4 g fiber, 31 g pro.
Daily Values: 86% vit. A, 38% vit. C, 4% calcium, 22% iron

Sweet and Spicy Country-Style Ribs

Three kinds of pepper—hot pepper sauce, ground red pepper, and black pepper—give these Chinese-style ribs their kick. Serve over rice or in toasted sesame-topped buns.

Prep: 15 minutes **Cook:** 8 to 10 hours **Serves:** 8 to 10

3½ pounds pork country-style ribs
6 green onions, chopped
¼ cup reduced-sodium soy sauce
¼ cup molasses
2 tablespoons hoisin sauce
2 tablespoons brown sugar
2 tablespoons white wine vinegar
2 teaspoons toasted sesame oil
2 teaspoons lemon juice
½ teaspoon bottled hot pepper sauce
½ teaspoon ground ginger
½ teaspoon garlic powder
½ teaspoon chili powder
¼ teaspoon ground red pepper
¼ teaspoon ground black pepper
2 cups hot cooked rice

1 Place ribs in a 3½- or 4-quart crockery cooker, cutting as necessary to fit.

2 For sauce, in a small bowl combine green onions, soy sauce, molasses, hoisin sauce, brown sugar, vinegar, toasted sesame oil, lemon juice, hot pepper sauce, ginger, garlic powder, chili powder, ground red pepper, and ground black pepper. Pour the sauce over the ribs in cooker, turning to coat.

3 Cover and cook on low-heat setting for 8 to 10 hours or on high-heat setting for 4 to 5 hours. Transfer ribs to a serving platter. Strain sauce into a glass measuring cup; skim off fat. Serve sauce over ribs and hot cooked rice.

Nutrition Facts per serving: 329 cal., 13 g total fat (4 g sat. fat), 73 mg chol., 406 mg sodium, 27 g carbo., 1 g fiber, 24 g pro.
Daily Values: 3% vit. A, 6% vit. C, 6% calcium, 15% iron

Sweet and Spicy Country-Style Rib Sandwiches: Prepare the ribs as directed, except omit the hot cooked rice. Remove the cooked meat from the bones. Using 2 forks, pull meat apart into shreds. To serve, add meat to toasted, large sesame buns or kaiser rolls. Serve the strained sauce on the side. Makes 8 to 10 sandwiches.

Nutrition Facts per serving: 435 cal., 15 g total fat (5 g sat. fat), 73 mg chol., 717 mg sodium, 44 g carbo., 1 g fiber, 29 g pro.
Daily Values: 3% vit. A, 6% vit. C, 11% calcium, 21% iron

Pork Chops with Orange Sauce ♥

Orange marmalade and mustard team up for a glistening, tangy sauce to top chops and wedges of winter squash. Steam green beans or asparagus to serve on the side.

Prep: 20 minutes **Cook:** 5 to 6 hours **Serves:** 6

2 small or medium acorn squash (1½ to 2 pounds total)

1 large onion, halved lengthwise and sliced

6 pork chops (with bone), cut ¾ inch thick (2½ to 2¾ pounds total)

½ cup chicken broth

⅓ cup orange marmalade

1 tablespoon honey mustard or Dijon-style mustard

1 teaspoon dried marjoram or thyme, crushed

¼ teaspoon pepper

2 tablespoons cornstarch

2 tablespoons cold water

1 Cut squash in half lengthwise. Remove and discard seeds and membranes. Cut each squash half into three wedges. In a 5- to 6-quart crockery cooker place squash and onion. Trim fat from chops. Place chops on top of squash and onion.

2 In a bowl stir together broth, marmalade, mustard, marjoram or thyme, and pepper. Pour broth mixture over chops and vegetables.

3 Cover and cook on low-heat setting for 5 to 6 hours or on high-heat setting for 2½ to 3 hours. Using a large slotted spoon, transfer chops and vegetables from cooker to platter, reserving juices; cover meat and vegetables to keep warm.

4 For sauce, strain cooking juices into a glass measuring cup; skim off fat. Measure 1¾ cups juices, adding water if necessary. Pour juices into a medium saucepan. Combine cornstarch and the cold water; stir into juices in saucepan. Cook and stir over medium heat until thickened and bubbly; cook and stir for 2 minutes more. Serve chops with vegetables and sauce.

Nutrition Facts per serving: 265 cal., 8 g total fat (3 g sat. fat), 65 mg chol., 168 mg sodium, 27 g carbo., 3 g fiber, 21 g pro.
Daily Values: 3% vit. A, 20% vit. C, 7% calcium, 10% iron

Spicy Peanut Pork Chops

A creamy peanut sauce spiked with crushed red pepper cloaks these fork-tender chops. Be sure to use unsweetened coconut milk, which you'll find in the Asian foods section of your supermarket.

Prep: 20 minutes **Cook:** 6 to 8 hours **Serves:** 8

8   boneless pork chops, cut
       ¾ inch thick (about
       2 pounds total)
1   tablespoon cooking oil
2   cups shredded carrots
2   medium onions, chopped
       (1 cup)
1   14-ounce can light
       coconut milk
½   cup chicken broth
½   cup creamy peanut butter
½   teaspoon crushed red
       pepper
6   cups hot cooked basmati
       rice or shredded
       Chinese cabbage
       (Napa)

1 In a large skillet brown pork chops, half at a time, on both sides in hot oil.

2 In a 3½- or 4-quart crockery cooker place carrots and onions. In a bowl combine coconut milk, chicken broth, peanut butter, and red pepper; pour over vegetables. Place browned chops on top of vegetables.

3 Cover and cook on low-heat setting for 6 to 8 hours or on high-heat setting for 3 to 4 hours. Serve with rice or cabbage.

Nutrition Facts per serving: 500 cal., 18 g total fat (6 g sat. fat), 62 mg chol., 212 mg sodium, 47 g carbo., 3 g fiber, 32 g pro.
Daily Values: 78% vit. A, 7% vit. C, 6% calcium, 12% iron

trimming and skimming

Crockery cooker cooking requires little fat thanks to its low, moist heat. For low-fat meals I choose lean cuts of meat and trim away as much visible fat as possible. For poultry I remove the skin before cooking. I also brown the meat in a nonstick skillet sprayed with nonstick cooking spray.

Before serving the meal, I use a slotted spoon to transfer the meat and vegetables to a serving platter. Then I pour the cooking liquid into a glass measuring cup and let it stand for a minute or two. Once the fat rises to the top, I skim off any visible fat with a metal spoon.

Jill Moberly

Test Kitchen Home Economist

Greek Lamb with Spinach and Orzo

The sunny flavors of the Mediterranean come alive in this robust dish which features chunks of lamb tossed with spinach, orzo, and feta cheese.

Prep: 20 minutes **Cook:** 8 to 10 hours plus 5 minutes **Serves:** 8

1 3- to 3½-pound lamb
     shoulder roast (bone-in)
1 tablespoon dried oregano,
     crushed
1 tablespoon finely
     shredded lemon peel
4 cloves garlic, minced
¼ teaspoon salt
¼ cup lemon juice
1 10-ounce bag prewashed
     fresh spinach, chopped
5 cups cooked orzo
4 ounces crumbled feta
     cheese

1 Trim fat from roast. Cut roast to fit into a 3½- to 6-quart crockery cooker. In a small bowl combine oregano, lemon peel, garlic, and salt. Sprinkle evenly over sides of lamb roast; rub lightly with fingers. Place lamb in crockery cooker. Sprinkle lamb with lemon juice.

2 Cover and cook on low-heat setting for 8 to 10 hours or on high-heat setting for 4 to 5 hours.

3 Remove lamb from cooker. Remove meat from bones; discard bones and fat. Chop meat; set aside. Add spinach to cooking juices in cooker, stirring until spinach is wilted. Add cooked orzo, feta, and lamb; stir to mix.

Nutrition Facts per serving: 409 cal., 16 g total fat (7 g sat. fat), 120 mg chol., 338 mg sodium, 25 g carbo., 5 g fiber, 38 g pro.
Daily Values: 20% vit. A, 17% vit. C, 14% calcium, 34% iron

Lamb Shanks with Barley ♥

Perfect for a simple Sunday supper, the lamb shanks cook while you take a hike in the woods, play a game of tag football, or snuggle up to watch a favorite movie on TV.

Prep: 20 minutes **Cook:** 7 to 9 hours **Serves:** 6 to 8

3 to 3½ pounds lamb shanks or beef shank crosscuts
1 tablespoon cooking oil
1 cup regular barley
1 medium onion, chopped
4 carrots, cut into ½-inch slices (2 cups)
3 stalks celery, cut into ½-inch slices (1½ cups)
1 14½-ounce can chicken broth
1 14½-ounce can diced tomatoes
⅓ cup water
½ teaspoon pepper
2 tablespoons balsamic vinegar (optional)

1 In a large skillet brown the lamb or beef in hot oil over medium heat. Drain off fat.

2 In a 5- to 6-quart crockery cooker combine barley, onion, carrots, celery, broth, undrained tomatoes, water, and pepper. Add lamb shanks.

3 Cover and cook on low-heat setting for 7 to 9 hours or until lamb pulls easily from bones and barley is tender. Transfer lamb to a serving platter. Skim off fat from vegetable-barley mixture. If desired, stir in balsamic vinegar. Serve with lamb.

Nutrition Facts per serving: 370 cal., 8 g total fat (2 g sat. fat), 99 mg chol., 529 mg sodium, 36 g carbo., 7 g fiber, 37 g pro.
Daily Values: 116% vit. A, 24% vit. C, 7% calcium, 24% iron

keeping meats warm

Few things are more satisfying than a piping-hot meal. To ensure that the meat and vegetables stay warm while I thicken the gravy or make a sauce, I always warm the platter or serving dish by running it under hot water and drying it quickly with a towel. Then I arrange the meat and vegetables on the platter and cover it with foil while I make the sauce.

Maryellyn Krantz

Test Kitchen Home Economist

Poultry

Chicken and Shrimp
Jambalaya

In This Chapter:

Chicken Curry ♥

An intriguing blend of coriander, ginger, turmeric, cinnamon, and red pepper makes this chicken and potato dish sizzle with flavors typical of Indian cuisine.

Prep: 30 minutes **Cook:** 8 to 10 hours plus 15 to 20 minutes **Serves:** 5

  5 medium potatoes, cut into
      1-inch chunks
      (1½ pounds)
  1 medium green sweet
      pepper, cut into
      1-inch pieces (¾ cup)
  1 medium onion, sliced
  1 pound skinless, boneless
      chicken breast halves
      or thighs, cut into
      1-inch pieces
1½ cups chopped tomato
  1 tablespoon ground
      coriander
1½ teaspoons paprika
  1 teaspoon grated fresh
      ginger or ¼ teaspoon
      ground ginger
  ¾ teaspoon salt
  ¼ to ½ teaspoon crushed red
      pepper
  ½ teaspoon ground turmeric
  ¼ teaspoon ground
      cinnamon
  ⅛ teaspoon ground cloves
  1 cup chicken broth
  2 tablespoons cold water
  4 teaspoons cornstarch

1 In a 3½- to 6-quart crockery cooker place potatoes, sweet pepper, and onion. Place chicken on top of vegetables.

2 In a medium bowl combine tomato, coriander, paprika, ginger, salt, red pepper, turmeric, cinnamon, and cloves; stir in chicken broth. Pour over chicken pieces.

3 Cover and cook on low-heat setting for 8 to 10 hours or on high-setting for 4 to 5 hours.

4 If using low-heat setting, turn to high-heat setting. In a small bowl combine cold water and cornstarch; stir into mixture in cooker. Cover and cook for 15 to 20 minutes more on high-heat setting or until slightly thickened and bubbly.

Nutrition Facts per serving: 246 cal., 2 g total fat (0 g sat. fat), 53 mg chol., 609 mg sodium, 31 g carbo., 5 g fiber, 26 g pro.
Daily Values: 11% vit. A, 90% vit. C, 3% calcium, 14% iron

Chicken and Rice Burritos

Your tortilla options are no longer limited to flour and corn. Look for green spinach and orange chili flour tortillas in your grocery store.

Prep: 25 minutes **Cook:** 6 to 7 hours plus 5 minutes **Serves:** 6 to 8

1 medium zucchini
1 large green sweet pepper, cubed
1 medium onion, coarsely chopped
½ cup coarsely chopped celery
1½ pounds skinless, boneless chicken breast halves, cut into ½-inch strips
1 8-ounce bottle green taco sauce
1 teaspoon instant chicken bouillon granules
½ teaspoon ground cumin
1 cup instant rice
6 to 8 nine- to ten-inch spinach, chili, or plain flour tortillas
¾ cup shredded Monterey Jack cheese with jalapeño peppers (3 ounces)
2 small tomatoes, chopped
2 green onions, sliced

1 Cut zucchini in half lengthwise. Cut each half into ¾-inch slices. In a 3½- or 4-quart crockery cooker combine zucchini, sweet pepper, onion, and celery. Top with chicken strips. In a small bowl combine taco sauce, bouillon granules, and cumin. Pour over chicken.

2 Cover and cook on low-heat setting for 6 to 7 hours or on high-heat setting for 3 to 3½ hours. Stir in rice. Cover and let stand for 5 minutes.

3 Meanwhile, warm tortillas according to package directions. Divide chicken mixture among warmed tortillas. Top with shredded cheese, tomato, and green onion. Fold bottom edge of each tortilla up and over filling. Fold in the opposite sides until they meet. Roll up from bottom to encase the filling. If necessary, secure tortillas with wooden toothpicks.

Nutrition Facts per serving: 408 cal., 10 g total fat (4 g sat. fat), 81 mg chol., 735 mg sodium, 43 g carbo., 3 g fiber, 35 g pro.
Daily Values: 20% vit. A, 58% vit. C, 18% calcium, 19% iron

Thyme Chicken and Mushrooms ♥

This easy-to-serve dinner is rich in flavor and perfect for casual entertaining. Rent a video and invite friends over for dinner and a movie.

Prep: 25 minutes **Cook:** 7 to 8 hours **Serves:** 6

  5 cups sliced assorted fresh
     mushrooms, such as
     shiitake, button, crimini,
     and oyster
  1 medium onion, chopped
  ½ cup chopped carrot
  ¼ cup dried tomato pieces
     (not oil-packed)
  ¾ cup chicken broth
  ¼ cup dry white wine or
     chicken broth
  3 tablespoons quick-cooking
     tapioca
  1 teaspoon dried thyme,
     crushed
  ½ teaspoon dried basil,
     crushed
  ½ teaspoon garlic salt
  ¼ to ½ teaspoon pepper
  3 pounds chicken thighs or
     drumsticks (with bone),
     skinned
  4½ cups hot cooked plain
     and/or spinach
     fettuccine or linguine, or
     hot cooked rice

1 In a 4- to 5-quart crockery cooker combine mushrooms, onion, carrot, and dried tomato pieces. Pour chicken broth and wine over all. Sprinkle with tapioca, thyme, basil, garlic salt, and pepper. Place chicken pieces on top of vegetables.

2 Cover and cook on low-heat setting for 7 to 8 hours or on high-heat setting for 3½ to 4 hours. To serve, arrange chicken and vegetables over pasta or rice; spoon juices on top.

Nutrition Facts per serving: 360 cal., 7 g total fat (2 g sat. fat), 107 mg chol., 350 mg sodium, 39 g carbo., 3 g fiber, 34 g pro.
Daily Values: 28% vit. A, 9% vit. C, 3% calcium, 20% iron

Creamy Chicken and Noodles ♥

This crockery cooker version of the classic chicken and noodle casserole calls for reduced-sodium and reduced-fat condensed soup, making it healthier than the original and easier to fix.

Prep: 25 minutes **Cook:** 8 to 9 hours **Serves:** 6

2	cups sliced carrots
1½	cups chopped onion
1	cup sliced celery
2	tablespoons snipped parsley
1	bay leaf
3	medium chicken legs (drumstick-thigh portion, about 2 pounds total), skinned
2	10¾-ounce cans reduced-fat and reduced-sodium condensed cream of chicken soup
½	cup water
1	teaspoon dried thyme, crushed
¼	teaspoon pepper
10	ounces dried wide noodles (about 5 cups)
1	cup frozen peas

1 In a 3½- or 4-quart crockery cooker place carrots, onion, celery, parsley, and bay leaf. Place chicken on top of vegetables. In a bowl stir together soup, water, thyme, and pepper. Pour over chicken and vegetables.

2 Cover and cook on low-heat setting for 8 to 9 hours or on high-heat setting for 4 to 4½ hours. Remove chicken from cooker; cool slightly. Remove and discard bay leaf.

3 Meanwhile, cook noodles according to package directions; drain. Stir peas into soup mixture in cooker. Remove chicken from bones; discard bones. Cut meat into bite-size pieces; stir into mixture in cooker. To serve, pour chicken mixture over noodles; toss gently to combine. If desired, season with salt and pepper.

Nutrition Facts per serving: 406 cal., 7 g total fat (2 g sat. fat), 122 mg chol., 532 mg sodium, 56 g carbo., 5 g fiber, 28 g pro.
Daily Values: 127% vit. A, 60% vit. C, 6% calcium, 19% iron

the right thyme

Timing is everything when adding herbs during cooking. If you use a dried herb, add it at the beginning of cooking. If you use a fresh herb, add it at the end of cooking so it doesn't lose all its flavor and color during the long cooking time. Fresh rosemary is an exception because it can withstand long cooking time.

Chicken and Sausage Paella ♥

Saffron, one of the world's most expensive spices, gives Spanish paella an enticing flavor and characteristic yellow color. Turmeric offers an economical and equally delicious alternative.

Prep: 30 minutes **Cook:** 7 to 8 hours plus 5 to 10 minutes **Serves:** 6

2½ to 3 pounds meaty chicken pieces (breasts, thighs, and drumsticks), skinned
1 tablespoon cooking oil
8 ounces cooked smoked turkey sausage, halved lengthwise and sliced
1 large onion, sliced
3 cloves garlic, minced
2 tablespoons snipped fresh thyme or 2 teaspoons dried thyme, crushed
¼ teaspoon pepper
⅛ teaspoon thread saffron or ¼ teaspoon ground turmeric
1 14½-ounce can reduced-sodium chicken broth
½ cup water
2 cups chopped tomatoes
2 yellow or green sweet peppers, cut into very thin bite-size strips
1 cup frozen peas
3 cups hot cooked rice

1 In a large skillet brown chicken pieces, half at a time, in hot oil. Drain off fat. In a 3½- to 5-quart crockery cooker place chicken pieces, turkey sausage, and onion. Sprinkle with garlic, dried thyme (if using), pepper, and saffron or turmeric. Pour broth and water over all.

2 Cover and cook on low-heat setting for 7 to 8 hours or on high-heat setting for 3½ to 4 hours. Add the tomatoes, sweet peppers, peas, and fresh thyme (if using) to the cooker. Cover and let stand for 5 to 10 minutes. Serve over the hot rice.

Nutrition Facts per serving: 397 cal., 12 g total fat (3 g sat. fat), 101 mg chol., 608 mg sodium, 35 g carbo., 2 g fiber, 36 g pro.
Daily Values: 8% vit. A, 109% vit. C, 6% calcium, 22% iron

Herbed Chicken with Potatoes

To peel the pearl onions, submerge the unpeeled onions in boiling water for about 3 minutes. Cut off the root end. Gently press the onions and the skins will slip off.

Prep: 25 minutes **Cook:** 7 to 8 hours plus 10 minutes **Serves:** 4

 8 ounces mushrooms, halved
16 pearl onions (about
       1⅓ cups), peeled
 ½ cup chicken broth
 ¼ cup dry red wine
 2 tablespoons tomato paste
 ½ teaspoon garlic salt
 ½ teaspoon dried rosemary,
       crushed
 ½ teaspoon dried thyme,
       crushed
 ¼ teaspoon pepper
 1 bay leaf
 4 small chicken legs
       (drumstick-thigh
       portion, about
       2 pounds total), skinned
 ¼ cup chicken broth
 2 tablespoons all-purpose
       flour
 2 cups hot cooked mashed
       potatoes (optional)
    Snipped parsley (optional)

1 In a 3½- or 4-quart crockery cooker place mushrooms and onions. Stir in the ½ cup broth, the wine, tomato paste, garlic salt, rosemary, thyme, pepper, and bay leaf. Add chicken.

2 Cover and cook on low-heat setting for 7 to 8 hours or on high-heat setting for 3½ to 4 hours.

3 Transfer chicken to a serving platter. Cover chicken and keep warm. For sauce, transfer vegetables and cooking liquid to a medium saucepan. In a small bowl combine the ¼ cup broth and the flour; stir into mixture in saucepan. Cook and stir until thickened and bubbly; cook and stir for 1 minute more. Remove and discard bay leaf. Spoon some of the sauce over chicken. Pass remaining sauce. If desired, serve with mashed potatoes and sprinkle with parsley.

Nutrition Facts per serving: 405 cal., 15 g total fat (4 g sat. fat), 109 mg chol., 687 mg sodium, 29 g carbo., 4 g fiber, 37 g pro.
Daily Values: 6% vit. A, 18% vit. C, 6% calcium, 16% iron

Garlic Chicken with Artichokes

Twelve cloves of garlic may sound overwhelming, but the garlic mellows as it cooks and imparts a delightful flavor to the chicken and artichoke hearts.

Prep: 20 minutes   **Cook:** 6 to 7 hours   **Serves:** 6

12	cloves garlic, minced
1	medium onion, chopped
1	tablespoon olive oil or cooking oil
1	8- or 9-ounce package frozen artichoke hearts
1	red sweet pepper, cut into strips
½	cup chicken broth
1	tablespoon quick-cooking tapioca
2	teaspoons dried rosemary, crushed
1	teaspoon finely shredded lemon peel
½	teaspoon ground black pepper
1½	pounds skinless, boneless chicken breast halves or thighs
4	cups hot cooked brown rice

1 In a small skillet cook garlic and onion in hot oil over medium heat, stirring occasionally, about 5 minutes or until tender. In a 3½- or 4-quart crockery cooker combine the frozen artichoke hearts, garlic mixture, sweet pepper, chicken broth, tapioca, rosemary, lemon peel, and black pepper. Add chicken; spoon some of the garlic mixture over chicken.

2 Cover and cook on low-heat setting for 6 to 7 hours or on high-heat setting for 3 to 3½ hours. Serve with rice.

Nutrition Facts per serving: 341 cal., 6 g total fat (1 g sat. fat), 66 mg chol., 159 mg sodium, 39 g carbo., 6 g fiber, 32 g pro.
Daily Values: 11% vit. A, 62% vit. C, 7% calcium, 10% iron

come for dinner

Looking for an easy dinner to share with friends after attending a game or some other activity away from home? For such occasions I pull out my crockery cooker and make a recipe that includes both meat and vegetables such as a pot roast, a thick soup, or a hearty stew. Before I leave for the event, I clean the greens and cut up vegetables for a salad I can toss together when we get back to the house. To keep dessert simple, I plan on ice cream and cookies.

Colleen Weeden
Test Kitchen Home Economist

Chicken Cacciatore ♥

Serve this Italian classic with plenty of pasta to sop up all the sauce. Like the traditional dish, this one is brimming with mushrooms, onions, and tomatoes, all perfectly seasoned with herbs.

Prep: 25 minutes **Cook:** 6 to 7 hours plus 15 minutes **Serves:** 8

2 cups sliced fresh mushrooms
1 cup sliced celery
1 cup chopped carrot
2 medium onions, cut into wedges
1 green, yellow, or red sweet pepper, cut into strips
4 cloves garlic, minced
3 pounds meaty chicken pieces (breasts, thighs, and drumsticks), skinned
½ cup chicken broth
¼ cup dry white wine
2 tablespoons quick-cooking tapioca
2 bay leaves
1 teaspoon dried oregano, crushed
1 teaspoon sugar
¼ teaspoon salt
¼ teaspoon pepper
1 14½-ounce can diced tomatoes
⅓ cup tomato paste
Hot cooked pasta (optional)

1 In a 5- to 6-quart crockery cooker combine mushrooms, celery, carrot, onions, sweet pepper, and garlic. Place chicken on top of vegetables. In a bowl combine broth, wine, tapioca, bay leaves, oregano, sugar, salt, and pepper; pour over chicken.

2 Cover and cook on low-heat setting for 6 to 7 hours or on high-heat setting for 3 to 3½ hours.

3 Remove chicken and keep warm. Remove and discard bay leaves. If using low-heat setting, turn to high-heat setting. Stir in undrained diced tomatoes and tomato paste. Cover and cook 15 minutes longer on high-heat setting. Spoon vegetable mixture over chicken. If desired, serve with pasta.

Nutrition Facts per serving: 214 cal., 6 g total fat (2 g sat. fat), 69 mg chol., 291 mg sodium, 13 g carbo., 2 g fiber, 25 g pro.
Daily Values: 0% vit. A, 37% vit. C, 5% calcium, 11% iron

Chicken and Shrimp Jambalaya ♥

If you like spicy Cajun food, use the Homemade Cajun Seasoning. The Cajun seasoning blend you buy in the supermarket is less fiery than our home-mixed three-pepper combo.

Prep: 20 minutes **Cook:** 5 to 6 hours plus 10 to 15 minutes **Serves:** 6

1 cup sliced celery
1 large onion, chopped
1 14½-ounce can low-sodium tomatoes, cut up
1 14½-ounce can reduced-sodium chicken broth
½ of a 6-ounce can (⅓ cup) tomato paste
1 tablespoon Worcestershire sauce
1½ teaspoons Cajun seasoning or 1 recipe Homemade Cajun Seasoning
1 pound skinless, boneless chicken breast halves or thighs, cut into ¾-inch pieces
1½ cups instant rice
8 ounces cooked, peeled, deveined shrimp with tails
¾ cup chopped green sweet pepper

1 In a 3½- or 4-quart crockery cooker combine celery, onion, undrained tomatoes, broth, tomato paste, Worcestershire sauce, and Cajun seasoning. Stir in chicken.

2 Cover and cook on low-heat setting for 5 to 6 hours or on high-heat setting for 2½ to 3 hours. Stir in rice, shrimp, and sweet pepper. Cover and let stand 10 to 15 minutes or until most of the liquid is absorbed and rice is tender.

Homemade Cajun Seasoning: In a small bowl combine ¼ teaspoon white pepper, ¼ teaspoon garlic powder, ¼ teaspoon onion powder, ⅛ to ¼ teaspoon ground red pepper, ¼ teaspoon paprika, and ¼ teaspoon black pepper.

Nutrition Facts per serving: 261 cal., 2 g total fat (0 g sat. fat), 118 mg chol., 391 mg sodium, 30 g carbo., 2 g fiber, 30 g pro.
Daily Values: 11% vit. A, 54% vit. C, 6% calcium, 22% iron

Hot Kielbasa and Potato Salad ♥

With the addition of turkey kielbasa, German-style potato salad becomes an ever-so-easy main dish. Serve with slices of pumpernickel bread.

Prep: 25 minutes **Cook:** 4 to 4½ hours **Serves:** 4

1 pound cooked turkey
  kielbasa or smoked
  sausage, cut into
  1-inch pieces
10 to 12 whole tiny new
  potatoes, halved or
  quartered
1 large onion, chopped
1 cup chopped celery
1 cup water
⅔ cup cider vinegar
¼ cup sugar
2 tablespoons quick-cooking
  tapioca
¾ teaspoon celery seed
¼ teaspoon salt
¼ teaspoon pepper
6 cups torn fresh spinach

1 In a 3½- or 4-quart crockery cooker combine sausage, potatoes, onion, and celery. In a bowl stir together water, vinegar, sugar, tapioca, celery seed, salt, and pepper. Pour over vegetables and sausage.

2 Cover and cook on high-heat setting for 4 to 4½ hours. To serve, divide spinach among 4 salad plates. Drizzle about 2 tablespoons of the cooking juices over the spinach on each plate. Using a slotted spoon, remove potatoes and sausage from cooker; arrange on top of spinach. Serve immediately.

Nutrition Facts per serving: 339 cal., 10 g total fat (3 g sat. fat), 70 mg chol., 1,227 mg sodium, 43 g carbo., 7 g fiber, 23 g pro.
Daily Values: 26% vit. A, 50% vit. C, 7% calcium, 34% iron

be prepared

Some meats and poultry store longer than others do. Products such as kielbasa, pepperoni, cooked sausage, and smoked meats and poultry stay fresh longer in your refrigerator. I find it helpful to keep one or two of these meats on hand along with the fixings for a recipe such as Hot Kielbasa and Potato Salad. If my plans change or I forget to thaw meat, I can always count on these meats being ready to go.

Kay Springer
Test Kitchen Home Economist

Fruited Turkey in Red Wine Sauce

Meaty turkey thighs simmer with prunes, dried apricots, and red wine for a rich yet mellow-tasting entrée. Serve with steamed green beans and buttery dinner rolls.

Prep: 30 minutes **Cook:** 6 to 7 hours **Serves:** 4 or 5

3 pounds turkey thighs
  (4 or 5 thighs), skinned
1 tablespoon cooking oil
½ cup pitted prunes
½ cup dried apricot halves
½ cup orange juice
¼ cup dry red wine
4 cloves garlic, minced
1 tablespoon honey
1 tablespoon finely
  shredded lemon peel
2 teaspoons dried thyme,
  crushed
½ teaspoon salt
1 tablespoon cornstarch
1 tablespoon cold water
  Hot cooked couscous or
  rice (optional)

1 In a large skillet brown turkey in hot oil. Transfer turkey to a 3½- or 4-quart crockery cooker. Place prunes and apricots on top of turkey.

2 Stir together orange juice, wine, garlic, honey, lemon peel, thyme, and salt. Pour orange juice mixture over turkey.

3 Cover and cook on low-heat setting for 6 to 7 hours or on high-heat setting for 3 to 3½ hours.

4 Using a slotted spoon, transfer turkey and fruit to a serving platter; cover turkey and keep warm. Pour cooking juices into a glass measuring cup; skim off fat.

5 For sauce, measure 1¼ cups juices. Transfer to a saucepan. Combine the cornstarch and cold water; stir into juices in saucepan. Cook and stir over medium heat until thickened and bubbly. Cook and stir for 2 minutes more. Spoon sauce over turkey. If desired, serve with hot cooked couscous or rice.

Nutrition Facts per serving: 539 cal., 17 g total fat (5 g sat. fat), 195 mg chol., 504 mg sodium, 35 g carbo., 3 g fiber, 57 g pro.
Daily Values: 37% vit. A, 32% vit. C, 9% calcium, 38% iron

Sausage and Sweet Pepper Sauce

For a less spicy pasta sauce, use ground turkey in place of the hot Italian turkey sausage. Freeze any leftover sauce for another meal.

Prep: 15 minutes **Cook:** 8 to 10 hours **Serves:** 6 to 8

1½ pounds uncooked Italian turkey sausage

4 cups chopped, peeled tomatoes (6 large) or two 14½-ounce cans tomatoes, cut up

2 medium green and/or yellow sweet peppers, cut into strips

2 cups sliced fresh mushrooms

1 large onion, chopped

2 6-ounce cans Italian-style tomato paste

2 cloves garlic, minced

1 teaspoon sugar

½ teaspoon pepper

1 bay leaf

12 to 16 ounces dried penne, rigatoni, or other pasta
    Finely shredded Parmesan cheese (optional)

1 Remove casings from sausage, if present. In a large skillet cook turkey sausage until brown. Drain off fat. Transfer cooked sausage to a 3½- to 5-quart crockery cooker. Stir in fresh or undrained canned tomatoes, sweet peppers, mushrooms, onion, tomato paste, garlic, sugar, pepper, and bay leaf.

2 Cover and cook on low-heat setting for 8 to 10 hours or on high-heat setting for 4 to 5 hours.

3 Cook pasta according to package directions; drain. Remove and discard bay leaf from sauce. Serve sauce over pasta. If desired, sprinkle with Parmesan cheese.

Nutrition Facts per serving: 517 cal., 14 g total fat (4 g sat. fat), 60 mg chol., 1,394 mg sodium, 69 g carbo., 6 g fiber, 30 g pro.
Daily Values: 18% vit. A, 106% vit. C, 6% calcium, 37% iron

Turkey Meatballs and Gravy

Ladle the meatballs and lemon-scented gravy over mashed potatoes or noodles. For extra flavor, stir Parmesan cheese into the potatoes or toss the noodles with snipped fresh basil.

Prep: 45 minutes **Cook:** 6 to 8 hours **Serves:** 8

2 beaten eggs
¾ cup seasoned fine dry bread crumbs
1 medium onion, finely chopped
½ cup finely chopped celery
2 tablespoons snipped parsley
¼ teaspoon pepper
⅛ teaspoon garlic powder
2 pounds uncooked ground turkey
1 10¾-ounce can reduced-fat and reduced-sodium condensed cream of mushroom soup
1 cup water
1 0.87-ounce envelope turkey gravy mix
1 teaspoon finely shredded lemon peel
1 teaspoon dried thyme, crushed
1 bay leaf
4 cups hot cooked mashed potatoes or noodles
   Snipped parsley (optional)

1 For meatballs, in a bowl combine eggs, bread crumbs, onion, celery, 2 tablespoons parsley, the pepper, and garlic powder. Add ground turkey and mix well. Shape into 1½-inch balls.

2 In a large nonstick skillet brown meatballs, half at a time. Or, arrange meatballs in a lightly greased 15×10×1-inch baking pan; bake in a 350° oven for 15 minutes. Transfer browned meatballs to a 3½- or 4-quart crockery cooker.

3 In a bowl combine soup, water, gravy mix, lemon peel, thyme, and bay leaf. Pour over meatballs.

4 Cover and cook on low-heat setting for 6 to 8 hours or on high-heat setting for 3 to 4 hours. Remove and discard bay leaf. Serve with mashed potatoes or noodles. If desired, sprinkle with additional snipped parsley.

Nutrition Facts per serving: 390 cal., 16 g total fat (4 g sat. fat), 146 mg chol., 887 mg sodium, 34 g carbo., 2 g fiber, 26 g pro.
Daily Values: 8% vit. A, 40% vit. C, 10% calcium, 15% iron

Mexican-Style Sausage and Beans

Let the salsa—mild, medium, or hot—determine the hotness of this bean and sausage dinner. Serve with a pan of corn bread.

Prep: 15 minutes **Cook:** 6 to 7 hours **Serves:** 6

1	cup chopped green sweet pepper
1	large onion, chopped
3	cloves garlic, minced
1	15-ounce can white kidney beans (cannellini), rinsed and drained
1	15-ounce can black beans, rinsed and drained
1	15-ounce can red kidney beans, rinsed and drained
1½	cups frozen whole kernel corn
1½	cups bottled salsa
1	teaspoon ground cumin
1	pound smoked turkey sausage, sliced

1 In a 3½- or 4-quart crockery cooker combine sweet pepper, onion, garlic, white kidney beans, black beans, red kidney beans, corn, salsa, cumin, and sausage.

2 Cover and cook on low-heat setting for 6 to 7 hours or on high-heat setting for 3 to 3½ hours.

Nutrition Facts per serving: 307 cal., 8 g total fat (2 g sat. fat), 47 mg chol., 1,213 mg sodium, 47 g carbo., 12 g fiber, 28 g pro.
Daily Values: 3% vit. A, 44% vit. C, 8% calcium, 21% iron

beans on ice

Canned beans are easy to use and rich in fiber and protein, but they also deliver a healthy dose of sodium. Home-cooked dried beans offer all the nutrients of canned ones without all the sodium. They're also available in many more varieties. When I have time, I cook dried beans and freeze them in 2-cup portions. Whenever a recipe calls for a 15-ounce can of beans, I thaw a container of cooked beans to use instead.

Lori Wilson
Test Kitchen Home Economist

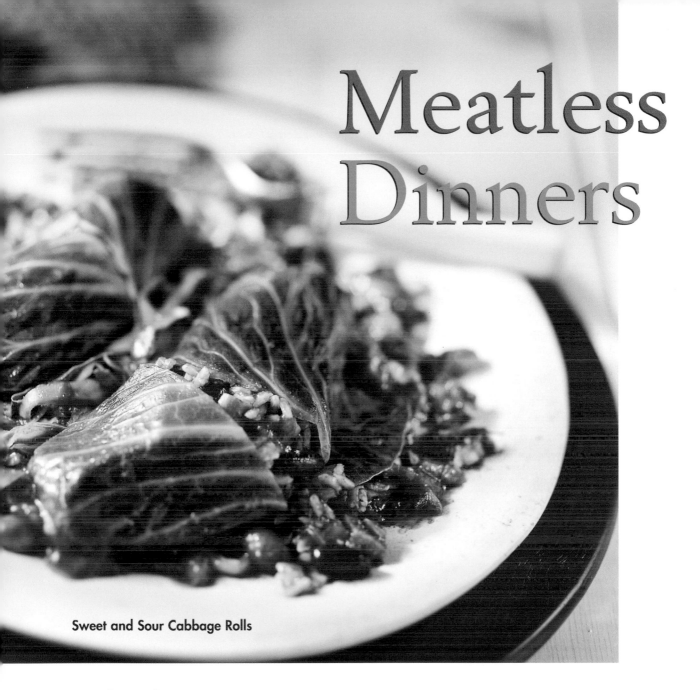

Meatless Dinners

Sweet and Sour Cabbage Rolls

In This Chapter:

Vegetable-Barley Medley ♥

Fix this mélange of vegetables and barley in late summer, when zucchini and tomatoes are at their peak. As a hot-weather bonus, the crockery cooker cooks without heating up your kitchen.

Prep: 20 minutes **Cook:** 7 to 8 hours plus 30 minutes **Serves:** 4

1   15-ounce can black beans, rinsed and drained
1   14½-ounce can vegetable broth or chicken broth
1   10-ounce package frozen whole kernel corn
1   large onion, chopped
½   cup regular barley
1   medium green sweet pepper, chopped (¾ cup)
1   medium carrot, thinly sliced (½ cup)
2   cloves garlic, minced
2   tablespoons snipped parsley
1   teaspoon dried basil or oregano, crushed
½   teaspoon salt
¼   teaspoon ground black pepper
1   medium zucchini, halved lengthwise and thinly sliced (1¼ cups)
2   medium tomatoes, coarsely chopped (1½ cups)
1   tablespoon lemon juice

1 In a 3½- to 5-quart crockery cooker combine drained beans, vegetable or chicken broth, corn, onion, barley, sweet pepper, carrot, garlic, parsley, basil or oregano, salt, and black pepper.

2 Cover and cook on low-heat setting for 7 to 8 hours or on high-heat setting for 3½ to 4 hours.

3 If using low-heat setting, turn to high-heat setting. Stir in the zucchini, tomatoes, and lemon juice. Cover and cook for 30 minutes more on high-heat setting.

Nutrition Facts per serving: 278 cal., 2 g total fat (0 g sat. fat), 0 mg chol., 1,001 mg sodium, 62 g carbo., 13 g fiber, 14 g pro.
Daily Values: 48% vit. A, 80% vit. C, 8% calcium, 17% iron

Black Beans and Rice ♥

This signature dish of Cuba and other Caribbean islands has soared in popularity stateside. It's just spicy enough to satisfy the American palate, is low in fat, and satisfies hungry appetites.

Prep: 20 minutes **Stand:** 1 hour **Cook:** 4 to 5 hours plus 15 minutes **Serves:** 4

2¼ cups dry black beans
    (about 1 pound)
  3 cups chopped onion
4½ cups water
  3 to 4 jalapeño peppers,
    seeded and finely
    chopped*
  6 to 8 cloves garlic, minced
  4 bay leaves
  1 tablespoon ground cumin
  2 teaspoons salt
  ½ teaspoon pepper
  2 cups instant brown rice
    Fresh cilantro (optional)
    Jalapeño pepper slices
      (optional)
    Lemon wedges (optional)

1 Rinse beans; place in a large saucepan. Add enough water to cover beans by 2 inches. Bring to boiling; reduce heat. Simmer, uncovered, for 10 minutes. Remove from heat. Cover; let stand about 1 hour. Drain and rinse beans.

2 In a 3½- or 4-quart crockery cooker combine the beans, onion, 4½ cups fresh water, chopped jalapeño peppers, garlic, bay leaves, cumin, salt, and pepper.

3 Cover and cook on high-heat setting for 4 to 5 hours. Remove and discard bay leaves. Stir in instant brown rice. Cover and cook 15 minutes more.

4 If desired, garnish with cilantro and serve with jalapeño pepper slices and lemon wedges.

Nutrition Facts per serving: 542 cal., 3 g total fat (0 g sat. fat), 0 mg chol., 1,189 mg sodium, 105 g carbo., 21 g fiber, 28 g pro.
Daily Values: 0% vit. A, 20% vit. C, 18% calcium, 36% iron

*Note: Hot peppers contain oils that can burn eyes, lips, and sensitive skin. Wear plastic gloves while preparing peppers and be sure to thoroughly wash hands afterward.

crockery beans

Your crockery cooker handily cooks dried beans to tasty tenderness. However, because beans cook more slowly in a crockery cooker than in a saucepan, the beans must be pre-cooked for 10 minutes instead of the 2 minutes typical of stove-top recipes. Soaking the beans overnight will not work for crockery cooker recipes because the beans will never become tender. Our recipes tell you exactly how to precook the beans for best results.

Scalloped Potatoes and Beans ♥

Kidney and black beans elevate scalloped potatoes from a supporting role to the main attraction. To cut down on prep time, leave the peels on the potatoes.

Prep: 15 minutes **Cook:** 8 to 10 hours **Serves:** 5

1 15-ounce can red kidney beans, rinsed and drained

1 15-ounce can black beans, rinsed and drained

1 large onion, chopped

2 stalks celery, sliced ¼ inch thick

1 cup frozen peas

1 large green sweet pepper, seeded and chopped

1 10¾-ounce can condensed cheddar cheese, cream of potato, or cream of mushroom soup

4 cloves garlic, minced

1 teaspoon dried thyme, crushed

¼ teaspoon pepper

1 pound potatoes, sliced ¼ inch thick

1 cup shredded cheddar cheese (4 ounces) (optional)

1 In a large bowl combine kidney beans, black beans, onion, celery, peas, sweet pepper, soup, garlic, thyme, and pepper.

2 Spoon half of the bean mixture into a 3½- or 4-quart crockery cooker. Top with the potatoes and the remaining bean mixture.

3 Cover and cook on low-heat setting for 8 to 10 hours or on high-heat setting for 4 to 5 hours. If desired, top each serving with cheddar cheese.

Nutrition Facts per serving: 287 cal., 5 g total fat (2 g sat. fat), 8 mg chol., 878 mg sodium, 55 g carbo., 14 g fiber, 18 g pro.
Daily Values: 15% vit. A, 67% vit. C, 14% calcium, 20% iron

Sweet and Sour Cabbage Rolls ♥

Raisins, lemon juice, and brown sugar transform purchased marinara sauce into a sweet and tangy sauce to drape over cabbage rolls filled with beans and rice.

Prep: 1 hour **Cook:** 7 to 9 hours **Serves:** 4

1 large head green cabbage
1 15-ounce can red kidney beans or black beans, rinsed and drained
1 cup cooked brown rice
½ cup chopped carrots
½ cup chopped celery
1 medium onion, chopped
1 clove garlic, minced
3½ cups marinara sauce or meatless spaghetti sauce
⅓ cup raisins
3 tablespoons lemon juice
1 tablespoon brown sugar

1 Remove 8 large outer leaves from head of cabbage. In a Dutch oven cook the cabbage leaves in boiling water for 4 to 5 minutes or just until leaves are limp. Drain cabbage leaves. Trim the thick rib in center of each leaf. Set leaves aside. Shred 4 cups of the remaining cabbage; place shredded cabbage in a 3½- to 6-quart crockery cooker.

2 In medium bowl combine beans, cooked rice, carrots, celery, onion, garlic, and ½ cup of the marinara sauce. Divide bean mixture evenly among the 8 cabbage leaves, using about ⅓ cup per leaf. Fold sides of each leaf over filling and roll up.

3 Combine remaining marinara sauce, raisins, lemon juice, and brown sugar. Pour about half of the sauce mixture over shredded cabbage in cooker. Stir to mix. Place cabbage rolls on top of the shredded cabbage. Top with remaining sauce.

4 Cover and cook on low-heat setting for 7 to 9 hours or on high-heat setting for 3½ to 4½ hours. Carefully remove the cooked cabbage rolls and serve with the shredded cabbage.

Nutrition Facts per serving: 429 cal., 12 g total fat (3 g sat. fat), 0 mg chol., 1,575 mg sodium, 72 g carbo., 17 g fiber, 13 g pro.
Daily Values: 123% vit. A, 118% vit. C, 17% calcium, 22% iron

Pasta with Eggplant Sauce ♥

With its mild flavor and spongy texture, eggplant soaks up flavors when cooked with other foods. Chunks of eggplant offer a low-calorie alternative to ground beef or sausage.

Prep: 20 minutes **Cook:** 7 to 8 hours **Serves:** 6

1 medium eggplant
1 medium onion, chopped
1 28-ounce can Italian-style tomatoes, cut up
1 6-ounce can Italian-style tomato paste
1 4-ounce can sliced mushrooms, drained
2 cloves garlic, minced
¼ cup dry red wine
¼ cup water
1½ teaspoons dried oregano, crushed
½ cup pitted kalamata olives or pitted ripe olives, sliced
2 tablespoons snipped parsley
4 cups hot cooked penne pasta
⅓ cup grated or shredded Parmesan cheese
2 tablespoons toasted pine nuts (optional)

1 If desired, peel eggplant. Cut eggplant into 1-inch cubes. In a 3½- to 5½-quart crockery cooker combine eggplant, onion, undrained tomatoes, tomato paste, mushrooms, garlic, wine, water, and oregano.

2 Cover and cook on low-heat setting for 7 to 8 hours or on high-heat setting for 3½ to 4 hours. Stir in olives and parsley. Season to taste with salt and pepper. Serve over pasta. Sprinkle with Parmesan cheese and, if desired, toasted pine nuts.

Nutrition Facts per serving: 259 cal., 6 g total fat (1 g sat. fat), 4 mg chol., 804 mg sodium, 42 g carbo., 7 g fiber, 10 g pro.
Daily Values: 18% vit. A, 37% vit. C, 13% calcium, 20% iron

Curried Vegetables and Rice ♥

To ease end-of-the-day preparations, cut up the cauliflower and zucchini in the morning. In the evening, just add them to the potatoes and carrots that have been cooking all day.

Prep: 15 minutes **Cook:** 8 to 10 hours plus 30 minutes **Serves:** 6

3	medium potatoes, cut into ½-inch chunks (3 cups)
4	medium carrots, cut into ¼-inch slices (2 cups)
1	large red onion, cut into strips
1¼	cups apple juice
2	tablespoons quick-cooking tapioca
2	teaspoons curry powder
1	teaspoon grated fresh ginger
½	teaspoon salt
½	teaspoon ground cardamom
1	cup uncooked regular brown rice
1	12.3-ounce package extra-firm tofu, drained and cut into ¾-inch cubes
1	medium zucchini, halved lengthwise and cut into ½-inch slices
1	cup frozen peas
⅓	cup golden raisins
	Chutney (optional)

1 In a 3½- or 4-quart crockery cooker combine potatoes, carrots, onion, apple juice, tapioca, curry powder, fresh ginger, salt, and ground cardamom.

2 Cover and cook on low-heat setting for 8 to 10 hours or on high-heat setting for 4 to 5 hours.

3 Cook rice according to package directions. If using low-heat setting, turn to high-heat setting. Add tofu, zucchini, peas, and raisins. Cover and cook for 30 minutes more. Serve vegetable mixture over hot cooked rice. If desired, serve with chutney.

Nutrition Facts per serving: 326 cal., 3 g total fat (0 g sat. fat), 0 mg chol., 262 mg sodium, 65 g carbo., 7 g fiber, 11 g pro.
Daily Values: 105% vit. A, 33% vit. C, 7% calcium, 17% iron

Vegetarian Chili with Pasta ♥

Be sure to chop the onion finely so it's completely cooked by the time you're ready to dish up bowls of this family-style dinner.

Prep: 20 minutes **Cook:** 4 to 5 hours **Serves:** 5

1 15-ounce can garbanzo beans, rinsed and drained

1 15-ounce can red kidney beans, rinsed and drained

2 14½-ounce cans diced tomatoes

1 8-ounce can tomato sauce

1 large onion, finely chopped

½ cup chopped green or yellow sweet pepper

2 cloves garlic, minced

2 to 3 teaspoons chili powder

½ teaspoon dried oregano, crushed

⅛ teaspoon ground red pepper (optional)

1 cup wagon wheel pasta or elbow macaroni
   Shredded cheddar cheese (optional)

1 In a 3½- or 4-quart crockery cooker combine the garbanzo beans, kidney beans, undrained tomatoes, tomato sauce, onion, sweet pepper, garlic, chili powder, oregano, and, if desired, ground red pepper.

2 Cover and cook on low-heat setting for 4 to 5 hours or on high-heat setting for 2 to 2½ hours.

3 Cook pasta according to package directions; drain. Stir cooked pasta into bean mixture. Serve in bowls and, if desired, sprinkle with cheddar cheese.

Nutrition Facts per serving: 273 cal., 2 g total fat (0 g sat. fat), 0 mg chol., 868 mg sodium, 53 g carbo., 10 g fiber, 14 g pro.
Daily Values: 13% vit. A, 57% vit. C, 13% calcium, 22% iron

Savory Beans and Rice ♥

Brown rice is the least-processed form of rice. Layers of bran are left on the kernels, giving them a tan color and chewy texture. Spoon these saucy red beans over a bed of nutty tasting brown rice.

Prep: 20 minutes **Stand:** 1 hour **Cook:** 9 to 10 hours plus 30 minutes **Serves:** 5

1¼ cups dry red beans or dry red kidney beans
1 large onion, chopped
¾ cup sliced celery
2 cloves garlic, minced
½ of a vegetable bouillon cube
1 teaspoon dried basil, crushed
1 bay leaf
1¼ cups water
1¼ cups brown rice
1 14½-ounce can stewed tomatoes
1 4-ounce can diced green chili peppers, drained
Few dashes bottled hot pepper sauce

1 Rinse beans; place in a large saucepan. Add enough water to cover beans by 2 inches. Bring to boiling; reduce heat. Simmer for 10 minutes. Remove from heat. Cover and let stand for 1 hour. Drain and rinse beans.

2 In a 3½- or 4-quart crockery cooker combine beans, onion, celery, garlic, bouillon, basil, and bay leaf. Pour the 1¼ cups water over all.

3 Cover and cook on low-heat setting for 9 to 10 hours or on high heat setting for 4 to 5 hours.

4 Cook brown rice according to package directions; keep warm. Remove bay leaf from bean mixture; discard. Stir undrained stewed tomatoes, chili peppers, and hot pepper sauce into cooked beans. Cook 30 minutes more. Serve bean mixture over hot cooked rice.

Nutrition Facts per serving: 323 cal., 3 g total fat (0 g sat. fat), 0 mg chol., 406 mg sodium, 74 g carbo., 10 g fiber, 16 g pro.
Daily Values: 4% vit. A, 22% vit. C, 11% calcium, 21% iron

bread ideas

What I love most about crockery cooker meals is that I need only bread and a salad or a fresh fruit or vegetable plate to complete the meal. I keep a supply of various baking mixes on hand so I can quickly bake up a batch of muffins or biscuits to serve with dinner. To add variety, I stir canned diced chili peppers into corn muffin batter or mix a little grated Parmesan cheese into biscuit mix.

Marilyn Cornelius

Test Kitchen Home Economist

Meatball and
Vegetable Stew

Five Ingredients

In This Chapter:

All-Day Pot Roast

Take 15 minutes in the morning to brown the roast, cut up the potatoes, and layer the ingredients in the crockery cooker. At the end of the day, gather the family for a vintage pot roast dinner.

Prep: 15 minutes **Cook:** 10 to 12 hours **Serves:** 5

1 1½-pound boneless beef eye of round roast or round rump roast

4 medium potatoes, quartered

1 16-ounce package peeled baby carrots

1 10¾-ounce can condensed golden mushroom soup

½ teaspoon dried tarragon or basil, crushed

1 Trim fat from roast. Lightly coat an unheated large skillet with nonstick cooking spray. Heat over medium heat. Add meat and brown on all sides.

2 Place potatoes and carrots in a 3½- or 4-quart crockery cooker. Place browned meat on top of vegetables. In a small bowl stir together soup and tarragon or basil; pour over meat and vegetables in cooker.

3 Cover and cook on low-heat setting for 10 to 12 hours or on high-heat setting for 5 to 6 hours. To serve, transfer meat and vegetables to a serving platter. Stir cooking juices in cooker; spoon over meat and vegetables.

Nutrition Facts per serving: 391 cal., 13 g total fat (5 g sat. fat), 79 mg chol., 567 mg sodium, 33 g carbo., 5 g fiber, 33 g pro.
Daily Values: 237% vit. A, 38% vit. C, 4% calcium, 19% iron

stocking up

Keeping my freezer and pantry stocked with some standbys helps my last-minute meal preparations go more smoothly and keeps me from making unnecessary trips to the grocery store. In the freezer, I keep a variety of frozen vegetables (to add to recipes or serve on the side), frozen fruit, and brown-and-serve rolls. In the pantry I stock up on packaged rice and noodle mixes, salad dressings, and muffin mixes to round out my meals.

Tami Leonard

Test Kitchen Home Economist

Beef with Mushrooms ♥

Cook a package of frozen mashed potatoes to serve with this saucy round steak. If you like, stir snipped fresh basil or grated Parmesan cheese into the cooked potatoes.

Prep: 10 minutes **Cook:** 8 to 10 hours **Serves:** 4

1 pound boneless beef round steak, cut 1 inch thick
2 medium onions, sliced
2 4½-ounce jars whole mushrooms, drained
1 12-ounce jar beef gravy
¼ cup dry red wine or apple juice

1 Trim fat from meat. Cut meat into 4 serving-size pieces. Place onion slices in a 3½- or 4-quart crockery cooker. Arrange mushrooms over onions; add beef. In a bowl stir together gravy and wine or apple juice. Pour over beef.

2 Cover and cook on low-heat setting for 8 to 10 hours or on high-heat setting for 4 to 5 hours.

Nutrition Facts per serving: 220 cal., 4 g total fat (2 g sat. fat), 51 mg chol., 814 mg sodium, 11 g carbo., 3 g fiber, 31 g pro.
Daily Values: 0% vit. A, 3% vit. C, 3% calcium, 20% iron

For a 5- to 6-quart cooker: Recipe may be doubled.

Corn and Sausage Chowder ♥

Welcome the family home on a blustery day with steaming bowls of this velvety-smooth soup. Cream-style corn and condensed soup provide the richness typical of a chowder.

Prep: 15 minutes **Cook:** 8 to 10 hours **Serves:** 6

1 pound cooked smoked turkey sausage, halved lengthwise and cut into ½-inch slices
3 cups frozen loose-pack diced hash brown potatoes with onion and peppers
2 medium carrots, coarsely chopped
1 15- to 16½-ounce can cream-style corn
1 10¾-ounce can condensed golden mushroom soup

1 In a 3½- to 5-quart crockery cooker place sausage, frozen potatoes, and carrots. In a medium bowl combine 2½ cups water, corn, and soup. Add to cooker.

2 Cover and cook on low-heat setting for 8 to 10 hours or on high-heat setting for 4 to 5 hours. Ladle into bowls. If desired, sprinkle with snipped fresh chives or parsley.

Nutrition Facts per serving: 238 cal., 8 g total fat (2 g sat. fat), 53 mg chol., 1,280 mg sodium, 28 g carbo., 2 g fiber, 15 g pro.
Daily Values: 58% vit. A, 38% vit. C, 2% calcium, 8% iron

French Dips with Portobellos

Slices of meaty portobello mushrooms give a savory new twist to French dip sandwiches. Pour the seasoned broth into individual bowls just large enough to dunk a corner of the sandwich.

Prep: 25 minutes **Cook:** 8 to 9 hours **Stand:** 10 minutes **Serves:** 8

1   3- to 3½-pound beef bottom round or rump roast

4   portobello mushrooms (3 to 4 inches in diameter)

1   large red onion, cut into ½-inch slices

1   14½-ounce can beef broth seasoned with onion

8   hoagie buns, split and toasted

1 Trim fat from roast. Cut roast to fit into a 3½- to 6-quart crockery cooker. Coat a cold large skillet with nonstick cooking spray; preheat skillet over medium heat. Brown meat on all sides in hot skillet. Drain off fat. Transfer meat to cooker.

2 Clean mushrooms; remove and discard stems. Cut mushrooms into ¼-inch slices. Place mushrooms and onion in cooker. Pour broth over meat and vegetables.

3 Cover and cook on low-heat setting for 8 to 9 hours or on high-heat setting for 4 to 4½ hours. Remove meat from cooker; cover and let stand for 10 minutes.

4 Meanwhile, using a slotted spoon, remove mushrooms and onion; set aside. Thinly slice the meat. Arrange meat, mushroom, and onion slices on toasted buns. Pour cooking juices into a glass measuring cup; skim off fat. Drizzle a little of the juices onto each sandwich and pour the remaining juices into individual bowls; serve with sandwiches for dipping.

Nutrition Facts per serving: 772 cal., 32 g total fat (10 g sat. fat), 106 mg chol., 953 mg sodium, 75 g carbo., 4 g fiber, 47 g pro.
Daily Values: 0% vit. A, 2% vit. C, 11% calcium, 43% iron

Apricot-Glazed Pork Roast ♥

You will have plenty of mustard-spiked apricot sauce to spoon over the succulent slices of pork roast. Cook some rice to serve on the side and soak up the extra sauce.

Prep: 15 minutes **Cook:** 10 to 12 hours **Serves:** 6 to 8

1 3- to 3½-pound boneless pork shoulder roast
1 18-ounce jar apricot preserves
¼ cup chicken broth
2 tablespoons Dijon-style mustard
1 large onion, chopped

1 Trim fat from roast. Cut roast to fit into a 3½- to 6-quart crockery cooker. Place meat in cooker. In a bowl combine preserves, broth, mustard, and onion; pour over meat.

2 Cover and cook on low-heat setting for 10 to 12 hours or on high-heat setting for 5 to 6 hours. Transfer meat to a serving plate. Skim off fat from sauce. Spoon some of the sauce over meat. If desired, serve remaining sauce with hot cooked rice.

Nutrition Facts per serving: 456 cal., 10 g total fat (3 g sat. fat), 93 mg chol., 184 mg sodium, 61 g carbo., 2 g fiber, 29 g pro.
Daily Values: 0% vit. A, 17% vit. C, 5% calcium, 13% iron

Thyme and Garlic Chicken Breasts ♥

These fork-tender chicken breasts are so rich in flavor that no one will believe you started with just five ingredients. Serve with rice pilaf and steamed broccoli flowerets.

Prep: 15 minutes **Cook:** 5 to 6 hours plus 10 minutes **Serves:** 6 to 8

6 cloves garlic, minced
1½ teaspoons dried thyme, crushed
3 to 4 pounds whole chicken breasts (with bone), halved and skinned
¼ cup orange juice
1 tablespoon balsamic vinegar

1 Sprinkle garlic and thyme over chicken. Place chicken pieces in a 3½- or 4-quart crockery cooker. Pour orange juice and vinegar over chicken.

2 Cover and cook on low-heat setting for 5 to 6 hours or on high-heat setting for 2½ to 3 hours.

3 Remove chicken from cooker; cover and keep warm. Skim off fat from cooking juices. Strain juices into a saucepan. Bring to boiling; reduce heat. Boil gently, uncovered, for 10 minutes or until reduced to 1 cup. Pass juices to spoon over chicken.

Nutrition Facts per serving: 178 cal., 2 g total fat (0 g sat. fat), 85 mg chol., 78 mg sodium, 3 g carbo., 0 g fiber, 34 g pro.
Daily Values: 2% vit. A, 13% vit. C, 3% calcium, 7% iron

Meatball and Vegetable Stew

Be prepared! To have all the fixings on hand for this hearty stew, stash a package of vegetables in the freezer and store a can of tomatoes and a jar of mushroom gravy in the pantry.

Prep: 10 minutes **Cook:** 6 to 8 hours **Serves:** 4

1   16- to 18-ounce package
      frozen cooked meatballs

½   of a 16-ounce package
      (about 2 cups)
      loose-pack frozen
      broccoli, corn, and red
      peppers, or other mixed
      vegetables

1   14½-ounce can diced
      tomatoes with onion
      and garlic or stewed
      tomatoes

1   12-ounce jar mushroom
      gravy

1½ teaspoons dried basil,
      crushed

1 In a 3½- or 4-quart crockery cooker place meatballs and mixed vegetables. In a bowl stir together tomatoes, gravy, basil, and ⅓ cup water; pour over meatballs and vegetables.

2 Cover and cook on low-heat setting for 6 to 8 hours or on high-heat setting for 3 to 4 hours.

Nutrition Facts per serving: 472 cal., 32 g total fat (14 g sat. fat), 87 mg chol., 1,883 mg sodium, 26 g carbo., 6 g fiber, 21 g pro.
Daily Values: 39% vit. A, 22% vit. C, 9% calcium, 21% iron

For a 5- to 6-quart cooker: Recipe may be doubled.

Chicken and Corn Bread Stuffing

No leftover chicken? Thaw a package of frozen diced cooked chicken or cut up a deli-roasted chicken to make this family-pleaser.

Prep: 15 minutes **Cook:** 5 to 6 hours **Serves:** 6

1 10¾-ounce can reduced-fat and reduced-sodium condensed cream of chicken soup or cream of mushroom soup
¼ cup margarine or butter, melted
1 16-ounce package loose-pack frozen broccoli, corn, and red peppers
2½ cups cubed cooked chicken
1 8-ounce package corn bread stuffing mix

1 In a very large mixing bowl stir together soup, melted margarine or butter, and ¼ cup water. Add frozen vegetables, chicken, and stuffing mix; stir until combined. Transfer mixture to a 3½- or 4-quart crockery cooker.

2 Cover and cook on low-heat setting for 5 to 6 hours or on high-heat setting for 2½ to 3 hours.

Nutrition Facts per serving: 387 cal., 14 g total fat (2 g sat. fat), 56 mg chol., 795 mg sodium, 41 g carbo., 2 g fiber, 23 g pro.
Daily Values: 16% vit. A, 52% vit. C, 3% calcium, 13% iron

Sweet and Sour Chicken ♥

For a dinner that's easier than takeout, fix this tasty one-dish dinner, bake frozen egg rolls for an appetizer, and add fortune cookies and sherbet for dessert.

Prep: 15 minutes **Cook:** 5 to 5½ hours **Serves:** 5

1 pound skinless, boneless chicken breast halves
2 9-ounce jars sweet and sour sauce
1 16-ounce package loose-pack frozen broccoli, carrots, and water chestnuts
2½ cups hot cooked rice
¼ cup chopped almonds, toasted

1 Cut chicken breasts into 1-inch pieces. In a 3½- or 4-quart crockery cooker combine chicken, sweet and sour sauce, and frozen vegetables.

2 Cover and cook on low-heat setting for 5 to 5½ hours or on high-heat setting for 2½ to 2¾ hours. Serve with hot cooked rice. Sprinkle with almonds.

Nutrition Facts per serving: 288 cal., 8 g total fat (1 g sat. fat), 53 mg chol., 425 mg sodium, 57 g carbo., 3 g fiber, 26 g pro.
Daily Values: 45% vit. A, 29% vit. C, 3% calcium, 13% iron

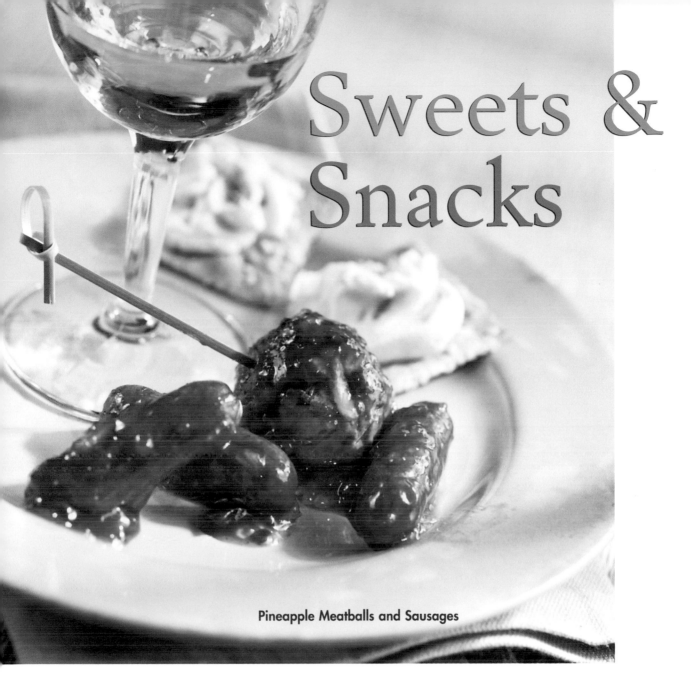

Sweets & Snacks

Pineapple Meatballs and Sausages

In This Chapter:

Hot Honeyed Spareribs

Party hearty with these ribs. They're perfect for an open-house appetizer party because they stay warm in the honey-sweetened picante sauce, and no one needs to go away hungry.

Prep: 20 minutes **Cook:** 6 to 7 hours **Serves:** 10 to 12

3½ to 4 pounds pork baby back ribs, cut into 1-rib portions
2 cups bottled picante sauce or salsa
½ cup honey
1 tablespoon quick-cooking tapioca
1 teaspoon ground ginger

1 Preheat broiler. Place the ribs on the unheated rack of a broiler pan. Broil 6 inches from the heat about 10 minutes or until brown, turning once. Transfer ribs to a 3½- to 6-quart crockery cooker.

2 In a medium bowl combine picante sauce or salsa, honey, tapioca, and ginger. Pour sauce over ribs.

3 Cover and cook on low-heat setting for 6 to 7 hours or on high-heat setting for 3 to 3½ hours. Skim off fat from sauce. Serve sauce with ribs.

Nutrition Facts per appetizer serving: 215 cal., 6 g total fat (2 g sat. fat), 43 mg chol., 246 mg sodium, 18 g carbo., 0 g fiber, 20 g pro.
Daily Values: 0% vit. A, 7% vit. C, 1% calcium, 4% iron

party time

Looking for an easy way to entertain? Host an appetizer buffet with the help of your crockery cooker. Start with one or two of the appetizer recipes in this section. If you want to make two recipes, borrow another cooker. Complement your crockery dishes with store-bought dips, chips, crackers, cheese, fresh fruit or vegetables, and a choice of beverages.

Buffalo Wings with Blue Cheese Dip

This sports-bar favorite is great when you and your friends gather to watch a football game on TV. Cold beer, celery sticks, and plenty of napkins are all you need.

Prep: 30 minutes **Cook:** 4 to 5 hours **Serves:** 32

16 chicken wings
　　　(about 3 pounds)
1½ cups bottled chili sauce
　3 to 4 tablespoons bottled
　　　hot pepper sauce
　1 recipe Blue Cheese Dip or
　　　bottled ranch salad
　　　dressing

1 Preheat broiler. Cut off and discard wing tips. Cut each wing into 2 sections. Place chicken on the unheated rack of a broiler pan. Broil 4 to 5 inches from the heat about 10 minutes or until chicken is browned, turning once. Transfer chicken to a 3½- or 4-quart crockery cooker. Combine chili sauce and hot pepper sauce; pour over chicken wings.

2 Cover and cook on low-heat setting for 4 to 5 hours or on high-heat setting for 2 to 2½ hours. Serve chicken wings with Blue Cheese Dip or ranch salad dressing.

Nutrition Facts per appetizer serving: 108 cal., 8 g total fat (3 g sat. fat), 21 mg chol., 217 mg sodium, 3 g carbo., 0 g fiber, 6 g pro.
Daily Values: 4% vit. A, 3% vit. C, 1% calcium, 2% iron

Blue Cheese Dip: In a blender container combine one 8 ounce carton dairy sour cream; ½ cup mayonnaise or salad dressing; ½ cup crumbled blue cheese (2 ounces); 1 clove garlic, minced; and 1 tablespoon white wine vinegar or white vinegar. Cover and blend until smooth. Store dip, covered, in the refrigerator for up to 2 weeks. To serve, transfer dip to a serving bowl. If desired, top dip with additional crumbled blue cheese.

Pineapple Meatballs and Sausages

Pinched for time? Instead of mixing and shaping the sausage meatballs, substitute a 16- to 18-ounce package of thawed, frozen meatballs and cook 3 hours or until the meatballs are heated through.

Prep: 35 minutes **Bake:** 15 to 18 minutes **Cook:** 2 to 3 hours **Serves:** 30 **Oven:** 350°

1 beaten egg

1 medium onion, finely chopped

⅓ cup finely chopped green sweet pepper

¼ cup fine dry bread crumbs

3 tablespoons soy sauce

1 pound ground beef

1 16-ounce package small cooked smoked sausage links

1 cup chopped green sweet pepper

1 12-ounce jar pineapple ice cream topping or pineapple or apricot preserves

1 cup hot-style or regular vegetable juice

1 tablespoon quick-cooking tapioca

½ to 1 teaspoon crushed red pepper

1 In a large bowl combine egg, onion, ⅓ cup sweet pepper, the bread crumbs, and 1 tablespoon of the soy sauce. Add ground beef; mix well. Shape into 1-inch meatballs. Place meatballs in a 15×10×1-inch baking pan. Bake in a 350° oven for 15 to 18 minutes or until no longer pink. Drain meatballs.

2 Transfer meatballs to a 3½- to 5-quart crockery cooker. Add sausage links and 1 cup sweet pepper. In a bowl combine ice cream topping or preserves, vegetable juice, remaining 2 tablespoons soy sauce, the tapioca, and crushed red pepper. Pour over meatballs and sausages; stir gently to coat.

3 Cover and cook on high-heat setting for 2 to 3 hours. Serve immediately or keep warm on low-heat setting for up to 2 hours more. Serve with toothpicks.

Nutrition Facts per appetizer serving: 124 cal., 7 g total fat (3 g sat. fat), 27 mg chol., 274 mg sodium, 10 g carbo., 0 g fiber, 5 g pro.
Daily Values: 2% vit. A, 11% vit. C, 1% calcium, 3% iron

Supreme Pizza Fondue

Mix all of these favorite pizza toppings in a crockery cooker and let them simmer for a while. When you're ready to eat, spear bits of focaccia to scoop up this pizza in a pot.

Prep: 20 minutes **Cook:** 3 hours plus 15 minutes **Serves:** 10

4 ounces Italian sausage

1 small onion, finely chopped

1 clove garlic, minced

1 28-ounce jar meatless spaghetti sauce

1 cup sliced fresh mushrooms

⅔ cup chopped pepperoni or Canadian-style bacon

1 teaspoon dried basil or oregano, crushed

½ cup sliced pitted ripe olives (optional)

¼ cup chopped green sweet pepper (optional)

Dippers such as focaccia or Italian bread cubes, mozzarella or provolone cheese cubes, or cooked tortellini or ravioli

1 Remove the casings from the Italian sausage, if present. In a large skillet cook the sausage, onion, and garlic until meat is brown. Drain off fat.

2 In a 3½- or 4-quart crockery cooker combine spaghetti sauce, mushrooms, pepperoni or Canadian-style bacon, and basil or oregano. Stir in the sausage mixture.

3 Cover and cook on low-heat setting for 3 hours. If desired, stir in ripe olives and sweet pepper. Cover and cook on low-heat setting for 15 minutes more. To serve, spear the dippers with fondue forks and dip into the fondue.

Nutrition Facts per appetizer serving: 254 cal., 12 g total fat (4 g sat. fat), 39 mg chol., 738 mg sodium, 24 g carbo., 0 g fiber, 13 g pro.
Daily Values: 18% vit. A, 31% vit. C, 15% calcium, 11% iron

Apple-Cherry Cobbler

Use sweet or tart dried cherries in this homey dessert. Tart cherries are a brighter red than the sweet ones, but either gives a pleasing flavor.

Prep: 20 minutes **Bake:** 8 to 10 minutes **Cook:** 6 to 7 hours **Serves:** 6 to 8

½ cup sugar
4 teaspoons quick-cooking
   tapioca
1 teaspoon apple pie spice
1½ pounds cooking apples,
   peeled, cored, and cut
   into ½-inch slices
   (4½ cups)
1 16-ounce can pitted tart
   cherries
½ cup dried sweet or tart
   cherries
1 recipe Spiced Triangles
   Ice cream, such as butter
   pecan or cinnamon;
   half-and-half; or light
   cream (optional)

1 In a 3½- or 4-quart crockery cooker stir together sugar, tapioca, and apple pie spice. Stir in the apple slices, undrained canned cherries, and dried cherries until combined.

2 Cover and cook on low-heat setting for 6 to 7 hours or on high-setting for 3 to 3½ hours. To serve, divide cherry-apple mixture among 6 to 8 shallow dessert dishes. Top with Spiced Triangles and, if desired, ice cream, half-and-half, or light cream.

Spiced Triangles: In a bowl combine 1 tablespoon sugar and ½ teaspoon apple pie spice. Unroll 1 package (8) refrigerated crescent rolls. Separate triangles. Brush tops with 1 tablespoon melted butter and sprinkle with sugar-cinnamon mixture. Cut each triangle into 3 triangles. Place on an ungreased baking sheet. Bake in a 375° oven for 8 to 10 minutes or until bottoms are lightly browned. Remove to a wire rack to cool.

Nutrition Facts per serving: 387 cal., 11 g total fat (3 g sat. fat), 5 mg chol., 333 mg sodium, 75 g carbo., 3 g fiber, 4 g pro.
Daily Values: 14% vit. A, 9% vit. C, 2% calcium, 10% iron

Fruit-and-Nut Bread Pudding

Indulge! This bread pudding is chock-full of dessert-time favorites: raisins, pecans, coconut, and candied pineapple. Add a drizzle of caramel ice cream topping for good measure.

Prep: 15 minutes **Cook:** 4 hours **Serves:** 6

  2 beaten eggs
 ½ cup sugar
 ½ teaspoon ground
     cinnamon
 ½ teaspoon vanilla
1½ cups whole milk,
     half-and-half, or light
     cream
  3 cups dry cinnamon-raisin
     bread cut into ½-inch
     cubes (about 6 slices)*
 ⅓ cup raisins
 ⅓ cup chopped pecans
 ⅓ cup coconut (optional)
 ⅓ cup chopped candied
     pineapple (optional)
 ½ cup caramel ice cream
     topping (optional)

1 In a bowl combine eggs, sugar, cinnamon, and vanilla. Whisk in milk, half-and-half, or light cream. Gently stir in bread cubes, raisins, and pecans. If desired, add coconut and pineapple. Pour mixture into a 1-quart soufflé dish (dish will be full). Cover the dish tightly with foil.

2 Pour 1 cup warm water into a 3½- to 5-quart crockery cooker. Tear off an 18×12-inch piece of heavy foil. Divide in half lengthwise. Fold each piece into thirds lengthwise. Crisscross the strips and place the soufflé dish in the center of the foil cross. Bringing up foil strips, lift the ends of the strips to transfer the dish and foil to the cooker. Leave foil strips under dish.

3 Cover and cook on low-heat setting for 4 hours or on high-heat setting for 2 hours. Using the foil strips, carefully lift dish out of cooker. Serve pudding warm or chilled with caramel ice cream topping, if desired.

Nutrition Facts per serving: 395 cal., 9 g total fat (2 g sat. fat), 79 mg chol., 63 mg sodium, 71 g carbo., 6 g fiber, 12 g pro.
Daily Values: 5% vit. A, 3% vit. C, 12% calcium, 17% iron

***Note:** To make dry bread cubes, cut bread into ½-inch square pieces. You'll need about 4 cups fresh bread cubes to make 3 cups dry cubes. Spread in a single layer in a 15×10×1-inch baking pan. Bake, uncovered, in 300° oven for 10 to 15 minutes or until dry, stirring twice; cool.

INDEX

Low-fat recipes indicated with a ♥.
Photographs indicated in **bold**.

Metric Cooking Hints

By making a few conversions, cooks in Australia, Canada, and the United Kingdom can use the recipes in this book with confidence. The charts on this page provide a guide for converting measurements from the U.S. customary system, which is used throughout this book, to the imperial and metric systems. There also is a conversion table for oven temperatures to accommodate the differences in oven calibrations.

Product Differences: Most of the ingredients called for in the recipes in this book are available in English-speaking countries. However, some are known by different names. Here are some common U.S. ingredients and their possible counterparts:
- Sugar is granulated or castor sugar.
- Powdered sugar is icing sugar.
- All-purpose flour is plain household flour or white flour. When self-rising flour is used in place of all-purpose flour in a recipe that calls for leavening, omit the leavening agent (baking soda or baking powder) and salt.
- Light-colored corn syrup is golden syrup.
- Cornstarch is cornflour.
- Baking soda is bicarbonate of soda.
- Vanilla is vanilla essence.
- Green, red, or yellow sweet peppers are capsicums.
- Golden raisins are sultanas.

Volume and Weight: U.S. Americans traditionally use cup measures for liquid and solid ingredients. The chart, top right, shows the approximate imperial and metric equivalents. If you are accustomed to weighing solid ingredients, the following approximate equivalents will help.
- 1 cup butter, castor sugar, or rice = 8 ounces = about 230 grams
- 1 cup flour = 4 ounces = about 115 grams
- 1 cup icing sugar = 5 ounces = about 140 grams

Spoon measures are used for smaller amounts of ingredients. Although the size of the tablespoon varies slightly in different countries, for practical purposes and for recipes in this book, a straight substitution is all that's necessary.

Measurements made using cups or spoons always should be level unless stated otherwise.

Equivalents: U.S. = U.K./Australia

⅛ teaspoon = 1 ml
¼ teaspoon = 1.25 ml
½ teaspoon = 2.5 ml
1 teaspoon = 5 ml
1 tablespoon = 15 ml
1 fluid ounce = 30 ml
¼ cup = 60 ml
⅓ cup = 80 ml
½ cup = 120 ml
⅔ cup = 160 ml
¾ cup = 180 ml
1 cup = 240 ml
2 cups = 475 ml
1 quart = 1 liter
½ inch = 1.25 cm
1 inch = 2.5 cm

Baking Pan Sizes

U.S.	Metric
8×1½-inch round baking pan	20×4-cm cake tin
9×1½-inch round baking pan	23×4-cm cake tin
11×7×1½-inch baking pan	28×18×4-cm baking tin
13×9×2-inch baking pan	32×23×5-cm baking tin
2-quart rectangular baking dish	28×18×4-cm baking tin
15×10×1-inch baking pan	38×25×2.5-cm baking tin (Swiss roll tin)
9-inch pie plate	22×4- or 23×4-cm pie plate
7- or 8-inch springform pan	18- or 20-cm springform or loose-bottom cake tin
9×5×3-inch loaf pan	23×13×8-cm or 2-pound narrow loaf tin or pâté tin
1½-quart casserole	1.5-liter casserole
2-quart casserole	2-liter casserole

Oven Temperature Equivalents

Fahrenheit Setting:	Celsius Setting*:	Gas Setting:
300°F	150°C	Gas Mark 2 (very low)
325°F	170°C	Gas Mark 3 (low)
350°F	180°C	Gas Mark 4 (moderate)
375°F	190°C	Gas Mark 5 (moderately hot)
400°F	200°C	Gas Mark 6 (hot)
425°F	220°C	Gas Mark 7 (hot)
450°F	230°C	Gas Mark 8 (very hot)
475°F	240°C	Gas Mark 9 (very hot)
Broil		Grill

*Electric and gas ovens may be calibrated using Celsius. However, for an electric oven, increase the Celsius setting 10 to 20 degrees when cooking above 160°C. For convection or forced-air ovens (gas or electric), lower the temperature setting 10°C when cooking at all heat levels.